Goblin Mode

How to Get Cozy, Embrace Imperfection, and Thrive in the Muck

McKAYLA COYLE

QUIRK BOOKS
PHILADELPHIA

Library of Congress Cataloging-in-Publication Data available upon request.

ISBN: 978-1-68369-353-6

Printed in China

Typeset in Fenwick, Goudy Modern MT St, Minion Pro, Calder, and HVD Bodedo

Designed by Paige Graff
Illustrated by Marian Churchland, except for stock illustrations by Arcanaofwaleson on pages 13, 17, 25, 27, 32, 45, 71, 93, 96, 98, 100, 102, 103, 129, 130, 135, 152, 154, 177–179, 181, 190, 191, and 200
Production management by John J. McGurk

Quirk Books
215 Church Street
Philadelphia, PA 19106
quirkbooks.com

10 9 8 7 6 5 4 3 2 1

For my family, who are all deeply and
wonderfully goblincore

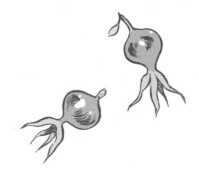

Welcome, Goblins

If you picked up this book, you're probably interested in getting in touch with your goblin nature—even if you're not sure yet what that means. You might be looking for more ways to connect with nature and feel present in the world. You might be looking for a community of nonjudgmental, curious people whose interests overlap with yours (however unconventional those interests may be). You might be tired of the constant performance associated with taste and style and looking for something that feels cozier and more representative of who you are. Whether you've been feeling one or all of these urges, the goblin life could be just what you're looking for.

We live in a culture that values perfection and conformity, so it can be difficult to feel like we have a place in the world if there's anything different about us. Our identities and relationships are boiled down to their simplest forms so that we're easier to digest. The goblin lifestyle pushes back against the idea that we must be clean and smooth and poreless in order to exist in the world. Dirty, sticky weirdos are just as deserving of love as anyone else. Our worth isn't dictated by how easy we are to advertise to.

But what do we mean by a goblin, exactly? To start with: well, you know, a goblin! A weird little guy from fairy tales and folklore. And from those weird little guys comes the inspiration for goblincore. *Goblincore* is a term that originated on social media to describe a particular combination of clothing, decor, and general outlook. Adding the *-core* suffix to the end of a word is a way to show that a particular clothing-decor-outlook combo is bound together by a taste or vibe. So goblincore is a set of tastes that feel inspired by or reminiscent of goblins. What kinds of things are reminiscent of goblins? Anything goblins love, like mushrooms, mud, and bugs. Goblincore is an aesthetic for those of us who are a bit too disorganized for minimalism, a bit too grungy for hygge, and probably a bit too sticky for anything else.

If any of that sounds interesting, exciting, or familiar to you, then you've picked up the right book. In these pages, you'll learn about how to incorporate a goblin spirit into your everyday life. From exercises to keep your observational skills sharp, to crafts that bring more goblin style into your life, to fashion and decor tips that will bring goblin-y goodness to your home and closet, this book offers all kinds of advice and activities to help you unlock your inner goblin. Are you interested in spending more time outside, or spending more time on your outfits? Would you rather learn to forage or learn about frogs? In here, you don't have to choose! Learn about any and all of the weird hobbies and unexpected interests that your goblin heart desires.

This is all to say that the goblin life is for everyone. It can be as simple or complex as you want to make it, and ultimately it's up to you to decide what kind of goblin you want to be. The goblin world welcomes everyone, and it has a lot to teach us about how to create a more inclusive, interesting world. Embracing your inner goblin means embracing the things that we're taught to ignore about human nature: the good, the weird, and the sticky. It's about getting back in touch with our inner child and giving that child the steering wheel. If any of this sounds good to you, you might just be a goblin.

CHAPTER 1

Our Goblins, Ourselves

Why we long for
the goblin life

Have you ever found yourself scrolling through the social media app of your choice, looking at photo after photo of beige paint, bare walls, tastefully understated furniture, and rooms with a single monstera or fiddle-leaf fig in the corner, and asked yourself, "Is this what it means to be an adult? Is this the only way to show people that I have Taste with a capital T? Is minimalism the only acceptable trend?" The answer, luckily, is *of course not.*

While minimalism can look beautiful and feel authentic to a lot of people, it's not for everyone. If you're the type of person who prefers a "lived-in" (read: messy) home, who prefers curated clutter to spotless chic, who has a lot of hobbies and interests that you like to display proudly instead of tuck away, you've probably had a hard time trying to fit into trends that prioritize a pared-down aesthetic. But that's okay! Your tastes are so much bigger than a single trend—no one can find their entire self in a style of interior design. People are way too complicated for that.

Being a goblin is about opening yourself up to the fact that you contain multitudes, and realizing that all of those multitudes deserve to be celebrated. Whether you celebrate them through redecorating your home, dressing yourself in an eccentric style, setting aside time to do things you love, or finding new ways to care for yourself, you don't have to minimize yourself because you feel the need to conform to a trend. As you'll learn, the goblin lifestyle encourages weirdness, celebrates clutter, and, above all, advocates for finding empowerment in your own comfort and happiness. So why continue trying to fit yourself into a lifestyle that doesn't suit you, when you could go goblin instead?

Goblins are interested in collecting cool trinkets, in finding furniture that allows for both nesting and burrowing. Goblins love nature, but the weird parts of nature. Goblincore is moss and mushrooms and snails. Goblincore is the cozy, homey aesthetic that welcomes everyone, including and especially weirdos. Goblincore has gathered up coziness, offbeat sensibilities, DIY skills, and affinity for nature and wadded them together into a big, soft moss ball. In the process it also took some established ideas about style and taste and turned them on their head.

But goblincore is more than just a decorating style. It's also a thriving online community for people who don't always fit in. Society is often reductive in its understanding of the huge range of human experiences, and it can be isolating to feel like a single mushroom sprouting up in a carefully manicured lawn. The goblin community welcomes everyone who's ever felt left out because of their identity, ability, race, class, or interests. Living the goblin life means reclaiming all the passions and interests you've ignored because they were too "weird" and honoring the things about yourself that made you feel like an outsider.

Goblins are weirdos who appreciate other weirdos. They love the things that other people dislike or take for granted. They elevate the strange and seemingly inconsequential to the status of cool, or even beloved. Goblins are tastemakers and trendsetters; they flout the rules of style, of utility, of gender and capitalism. Goblins live by the credo that one man's trash should be everyone's treasure. Who wouldn't want to be a goblin?

Who Can Be a Goblin?

Anyone! If you want to be a goblin, you're a goblin. Of course, the types of people who want to be goblins tend to be a little more specific. (For some reason not everyone wants to be a fun little guy?) The goblincore community as it exists online is largely made up of neurodivergent people, members of the

LGBTQ+ community (especially trans and nonbinary folks), anti-capitalists, introverts, artists, nature lovers, fans of both Baba Yaga and Baby Yoda, people who know a lot about crows, goth gardeners, and other cool, if slightly fringe, people.

The goblin lifestyle tends to appeal to these populations because it uplifts everything that is peculiar and yet overlooked. It celebrates the strange and offers a welcoming space that wants to hear about all the weird little things you found on the ground today. The online goblincore community actively pushes back against a lot of social norms by appreciating the handmade and found over the manufactured and purchased, and things that are flawed and unusual over things that are classically beautiful. Because of this, groups that are often sidelined and marginalized can find a home among the goblins.

In the lawn of society, goblins have dug out a space for themselves and planted moss and wildflowers and mushrooms and crooked trees in the dirt where that overwatered grass used to be. Goblins are invested in creating a new world that's more inclusive (and also weirder and more chaotic and greener) than the one we have now. Anybody who supports that kind of world is welcome to call themselves a goblin.

Why Goblins?

Of all the mythical, magical forest dwellers, why choose goblins as a mascot? Simply put, it's because goblins fit these ideals of comfort and weirdness perfectly. Goblins are often considered members of a fairy subspecies, though they're generally portrayed as grimier and less refined than fairies and other mythical creatures; they are playful, rebellious, fantastical creatures with a special connection to nature. Goblincore is an aesthetic that strives to be weird, unconventional, magical, and natural. In this aesthetic, goblins become representations of a love for things that are, like the creatures themselves, strange, unconventionally attractive, and maybe a little disheveled.

In fairy tales and traditional stories, goblins are very connected to nature, but not to the parts of nature that other people consider desirable or pleasing. They prefer mushrooms and moths to flowers and butterflies. They feel a deep kinship with the parts of the natural world that are often overlooked, because goblins understand how it feels to be overlooked. As the most unusual branch of the fairy folk family tree, goblins are committed to uplifting all things strange and extraordinary.

Goblins also love finding beautiful objects to collect and share, but their definition of beauty is wide ranging and personal. They're redefining what it means for something to be a treasure or to be beautiful. Most people wouldn't consider keeping jars of dirt or dried plants or bundles of twigs around as decor, but goblins know that these strange objects can hold personal meaning and that beauty is in the eye of the beholder. They're not hoarding trash but rather using their unique sense of style to cultivate a community. For goblins, collecting special treasures is a great way to meet people with similar preferences and interests who will also enjoy their collections. It's a way to hone their tastes and expand their communities.

Because goblins are committed to collecting and championing ideas and items outside of trends and popular taste, they're also anti-capitalist icons. The clothing, decor, jewelry, and art embraced by the goblin community is largely free, found, or homemade. Being a goblin isn't about spending lots of money on new things but rather about finding beauty in the things that are already right in front of you. It's about reinterpreting what it means to be beautiful and what it means to be precious to someone.

Goblins are magical beings who understand the complexities of the world; they're rebels and troublemakers who push boundaries when they know it's the right thing to do. While other beings tend to shy away from the muck of life, goblins embrace it wholeheartedly. They don't see the world as simply as people sometimes do, and they know that everyone is more complex than an easily definable label can ever express. Goblins are weird and messy, and they thrive in the muddy, contradictory spaces that we don't always love about ourselves. They love turning over a simple gray stone and finding a world of brightly colored bugs scuttling through the dirt.

PopGobs (Popular Goblins)

Goblins have been represented in many different forms over the course of history, from medieval times to Shakespeare to *Labyrinth*. If you lift up a rock in any fairy tale, you're likely to find a goblin hiding there, along with some cool bugs. Goblins are the tricksters, the mischievous rebels, the catalysts for action of many well-known stories. But maybe you want to know more about the cultural history of goblins before you dive full-bore into living your own goblin truth—or maybe you're on the lookout for a goblin role model. No problem. Let's look at some of the more well-known goblins throughout history by playing "Which goblin are you?"

CLASSIC GOBLIN (FROM FAIRY TALES): You're a mischievous little guy. You love causing trouble and playing practical jokes. You're easily irritated, and when you get angry you have a difficult time controlling your temper. Sometimes this can result in you seeming more frightening than you really are, but at heart you're well-meaning and benevolent. You act according to your own set of rules, but that doesn't mean your rules aren't thoughtful and pragmatic (at least, they seem that way to you).

PUCK (FROM WILLIAM SHAKESPEARE'S *A MIDSUMMER NIGHT'S DREAM*): Like the fairy tale goblin, you delight in playing pranks and causing mischief. However, you don't have great attention to detail and you often get distracted while doing tasks (even important ones). This might be because you have serious main character syndrome and you're too busy thinking about your next big line to focus on someone else's life. Or it might be because your priorities are a little different than those of others and you'd rather spend time having fun than doing someone else's bidding.

DISCWORLD GOBLIN (FROM TERRY PRATCHETT'S FANTASY NOVELS): You're as smart as you are weird, which is impressive, because you're super weird. However, you take great pride in your unorthodox interests and eccentric hobbies and people have learned to respect you for this. Unlike other goblin types, you have a mind for detail and mechanics, and you use these talents for good (mostly).

JARETH, THE GOBLIN KING (FROM THE MOVIE *LABYRINTH*): You've got an undeniable charm, and even the people who don't want to like you still find themselves drawn to you. Like other goblins, you're a rebel and a troublemaker, but unlike other goblins, you've got the allure of a Romantic hero. You are also, most importantly, the most dramatic person to ever live. Many goblins have a flair for drama, but nobody matches you when it comes to sheer spectacle.

THE GREEN GOBLIN (FROM MARVEL COMIC BOOKS): You really hate Spider-Man, and also you're Willem Dafoe, and also you have a pretty sick hoverboard. Unfortunately, you do have to meet all of these criteria in order to be the Green Goblin.

No matter which goblin you connected the most with, you might have noticed that these different depictions of goblins have a lot in common. These goblins are largely mischievous (where do you think the word *puckish* came from?), playful, rebellious, and clever. The goblins here have a sense of fun that sometimes borders on dark, but generally they're able to walk the line between weird and sinister pretty expertly.

Related to this, it's also important to note that these goblins are all weirdos. That's central to being a goblin. Being a weirdo is basically goblin rule number one. Your personal brand of weird can vary—maybe you're more of a "knows every species of mushroom" goblin than a "really committed to working a vest into every outfit" goblin—but all goblins embrace their weirdness and wear it on their sleeve.

Goblin Problems

That said: the goblin as a fantasy figure has also had some unfortunate associations. Historically, the image of the goblin as a malicious, greedy, hook-nosed creature has been used as a caricature of Jewish people in order to spread hate and fear. (Just picture the goblins at Gringotts in Harry Potter. Those goblins are basically a template for antisemitic imagery: sharp teeth, hooked noses, clawed fingers, pointed ears, hostile, literally in charge of a bank. It's frankly shocking.) In uplifting goblins, it's also important that we acknowledge (and reject!) the ways goblin imagery has been used for antisemitic purposes. Goblincore is for everyone, and promoting hate and discrimination goes against the Goblin Code, which you'll learn about at the end of this chapter.

When you're looking to fantasy stories and art for your goblin role models, watch out for the following red flags:

- **Greedy**: Goblins are collectors, but they love sharing the things they find and involving the community in the joys of their collections. If a goblin is greedy or hoarding things, it might be tapping into antisemitic tropes.

- **Evil**: Goblins are cool, playful rebels—they are *not* evil! Sure, sometimes goblins can be lovable disruptors, or thoughtful nonconformists, but they aren't villains. Evil goblins in stories might be antisemitic, or they might just be bad role models, but either way we can give them a wide berth.

- **Dirty**: Sometimes goblins get a little muddy, and all good gardeners get soil under their fingernails, but that's different from being dirty or unclean. An image of goblins that plays up their supposed unhygienic nature may be expressing antisemitism or some other type of xenophobia. (It's amazing how many different groups white America has portrayed as being unclean.)

If you're still concerned about goblins being antisemitic, take some time to read up on it! Different people will have different feelings, but it's up to you to listen and decide for yourself what feels right. It's harder to go wrong when you're making a thoughtful, informed choice.

The Goblin Look

At this point you might be wondering what it actually looks like to live a goblin lifestyle. Chances are, you're already closer than you think. The goblin community loves things like hand-knitted clothing (especially if that hand-knitting is less than perfect), cute glass jars full of mysterious items, crystals and dried plants, old books, herbs growing in recycled containers, candles dripping wax, animal bones, apothecary cabinets, and seashells. But if you're not into that specific look, maybe you're just not that kind of goblin! What's important is cozy clutter: being surrounded by *your* favorite familiar things, the things that make you feel at home, without worrying about being neat or presentable. To put it simply, a goblin lair feels like taking a walk in the forest and coming upon a clearing where the ground is really soft and mossy, and the clouds are just heavy enough to dim the sun, and the air is cool but not cold, and you've never considered going to sleep in the woods before but now you're not sure you ever want to sleep anywhere else.

To begin your journey to goblinhood, feel free to start small. Pile all your blankets on your couch or bed or floor before watching TV. Put on your three favorite, coziest articles of clothing (the less they match the better). Spend a day doing a simple craft like painting rocks or making a mushroom garland with paper and string. It doesn't take much to be a goblin, because goblins don't need much. The goblin life stresses the importance of finding beauty all around you, so you can probably decorate your whole space in goblin style without even going to a store.

Goblins love handmade items, so it may be useful to pick up a few crafting skills to add some extra flair to your goblin space. These skills don't need to be expensive—basically anything you need to know you can learn for free online (or at your local library), and many craft supplies can be found or made freely or cheaply if you know where to look.

Knitting and crocheting, gardening, molding things out of clay, embroidery, and making jewelry are hobbies that aren't too difficult to pick up and you can adjust them to your skill level pretty easily. (You'll learn some basic skills in this book!) If you're only okay at knitting, focus on making different kinds of scarves. If you like clay but don't want to go full kiln and pottery wheel, get some air-dry clay and make little mushrooms. Adorn your lair with things that are meaningful to you because they represent your passions and abilities. What's cozier than always being surrounded by little gifts you made for yourself?

To get you started on your goblin journey, here are some ideas for simple decorations you can make no matter your skill level. (In fact, the less skilled you are, the more goblin-y your crafts might turn out.)

- Cut paper (or felt) into mushrooms, then decorate them and glue them to a string to create a mushroom garland.

- Have any extra jars or glass bottles stored away? Break those out and fill each with a different item—it could be yarn, dirt, tea candles, crystals, whatever you have available.

- Blankets. Everywhere. This isn't really a craft project (unless you want to make your own blankets), but try belting or tying them around your body and call it "making your own clothes."

- Go for a walk and pick some flowers and leaves. Press them between paper under a thick book, or hang them upside down to dry out.

- Find old containers you aren't using anymore and fill them with dirt, then plant something in them.

- Use clay to make little frogs, mushrooms, moths, or rats so you have some friends in your space. If you don't have clay, you can draw them and hang the drawings on your wall.

Embracing a goblin style also means wearing clothes that reflect your goblin sensibilities. This doesn't mean you need to invest in a whole new wardrobe, but rather that you can rethink your clothing choices to maximize your comfort and emphasize your personal style. Here are some easy ways to start dressing like the goblin you are.

- Experiment with layering, and especially layering items you wouldn't normally think to wear together. Mix colors, patterns, and textures to find fun combinations that feel new and exciting.

- Make sure you feel comfortable in your clothes, both mentally and physically. Don't wear anything that makes you feel bad or self-conscious. If you prefer certain textures or fits, lean into that! Embrace comfort wherever you can find it.

- Accessorize! Put on all the rings and pins and patches and hats and bags and gloves you want. Carry a stuffed frog at all times. Only wear earrings you make yourself. There are lots of great ways to bring some goblinicity to your accessories.

- Upcycle, thrift, mend, and patch your clothes so that they'll last longer and look even more personalized. Not only are these methods good for the environment, they'll also take your style to the next level.

Of course, feel free to interpret goblinhood in the way that's the most conducive to your personal taste. If you don't like frogs or mushrooms, maybe incorporate more moss and rocks into your look instead. Don't feel bad if you need to switch things up a little to make your goblin nature work for you.

The Goblin Code

Now it's time to lay down the tenets of the goblin lifestyle. Goblincore is, obviously, an aesthetic and a style of decorating, but it's also much more than that. To be a goblin, there's a few ideas you'll want to embrace. This code isn't about creating rigid bylaws and enforcing punishment; rather, it's a loose structure that can guide you in your pursuit of a goblin life. Don't look at it as a set of absolutes. Instead, refer to this code when you're feeling out of touch with your goblin self, or when you're looking for direction in your goblin adventures.

No manifesto is ever truly comprehensive or complete, but this one highlights some of the most significant parts of goblin culture. Remember that the goblin life is all about making the world around you cozier, weirder, grimier, and more caring. Hopefully the following tenets can provide a useful base for that mission.

SEE BEAUTY EVERYWHERE

Perhaps easier said than done, but with practice even the most cynical goblin can restore their sense of wonder. Goblins can appreciate the traditionally beautiful, but what they really love is finding beauty in strange and unexpected places. Maybe there's a crack in the sidewalk that's shaped like a heart, or a childhood doll is starting to look a little haunted (in a good way). Maybe the dirt under a certain tree feels particularly cool and soft or the sound of the dishwasher is oddly soothing. Beauty doesn't look—or feel, or sound, or taste—one particular way. Part of the joy of being a goblin is getting to redefine beauty by your own standards, and then getting to spend every day of your life looking for glimmering moments of strange, surreal beauty.

EMBRACE YOUR WEIRDNESS

It should be obvious by now that goblins are weird. They're chaotic, charmingly feral little guys who live by their own rules. The goblin lifestyle is all about rejecting beauty norms and living your life the way you want to live it, so is it any surprise that goblins are weird? To truly become a goblin, you have to recognize the weirdness that's been in you all along. Double down on the interests your coworkers would be shocked to hear about. Dress in a way that truly feels good to you, not in a way that's socially acceptable. Explore new hobbies that you previously thought were unmarketable or maybe a little stinky.

Deep down, we're all weird. The goblin mindset is just about letting that weirdness rise to the surface and celebrating it. Your open weirdness could inspire someone else to embrace their secret weirdness. Or it might just make you feel more joyful and confident in your everyday life. Either way, when you're weird, you're winning.

GET COZY

This is one of the most important tenets of goblindom. There's not much about the adult world that's cozy or that allows any kind of personal comfort. We're largely expected to put aside what we want in favor of what society wants us to want. But that's a dumb way to live. If you're always cold in your office, you should be allowed to bring in three hoodies and a blanket. If wearing headphones to block out noise makes you feel safe, you should be able to wear headphones all day long. If you need to eat a snack every hour in order to function, you should always have access to delicious food. It's a privilege to be able to worry about things like coziness, but goblins are revolutionary in their belief that survival isn't something you have to earn and neither is comfort. Basic needs and small joys should both be in reach for everyone.

Coziness doesn't end at pillow forts and blanket nests (although those are a great place to start). Being cozy means making space for yourself. Goblins imagine a world where everyone's needs and interests are recognized, a radical new world where everyone can respectfully prioritize their own comfort.

CELEBRATE CLUTTER

Here's a strange phenomenon: we make, find, and buy pretty things only to hide them away in closets and cabinets and drawers and boxes. We're expected to be clean and tidy and presentable at all times, even in our own homes when we're alone. This doesn't make any sense. If you're someone who's messy by nature, why should you have to hide that messiness? Embrace it instead! Take out all the little objects that make you feel joy and place them around you so that you can look at them whenever you feel down. Surround yourself with the things you love, and keep them in plain view all the time. Clutter can be a great way of showing off what you love and caring about those loves openly. It's an opportunity to treat the things you love with tenderness and present them in a way that shows how much you care.

Goblin clutter isn't about randomly scattering things around (although you can do some of that if you want). It's about thoughtfully reflecting on the things you love and considering what they mean to you, then getting to display them in a way that reflects that meaning. It's all about really considering and celebrating the things you own, rather than thoughtlessly consuming. Surround yourself with items you love and you'll always be reminded of the little things that make you special and distinct. Goblin clutter is about allowing yourself to care for the things you have and finding joy and fulfillment in them.

BE A GOOD COMMUNITY MEMBER

No goblin is an island. Online, goblincore is known for being a welcoming and caring community, and that's because even the most introverted goblins know that being a goblin is better with other goblins by your side. Maybe your goblin community is also internet based, or maybe it's in person. Maybe your goblin community is a bunch of people who write old-timey letters to each other sealed with wax. Your community can look however you want it to, but having a community is going to bring so much more joy to your goblin experience than you would find if you went it alone.

So much of the goblin ethos is about pushing back against social and beauty norms and finding a new way through the world, and it's difficult to create a new world like this when you're alone. There are so many other wonderful goblins out there with great ideas and cool treasures, and they're all devoted to this fun, feral aesthetic that has a surprising amount of meaning and power in a late-stage-capitalist world. When you're interacting with other goblins, make sure to always offer them the care and respect you'd offer anything else in nature. Listen to others, note their boundaries, and speak with care. Being a goblin means understanding your part in a larger ecosystem and sometimes that ecosystem is a social one.

Also, make sure you're being a good community member to the people outside your goblin community. Find a way to use your particular set of goblin skills to improve the lives of those around you. Goblins are thoughtful, compassionate people and have a lot to offer their larger communities. If you know a lot about gardening, maybe help create a community garden in your area. If you're getting really good at knitting, make scarves or hats for your neighbors. You can start much smaller than this and just give your friends little goblin care packages (satch-

els of cool, tiny objects you've found). Any act of care can have a huge impact, and there are few things goblins love more than creating change (and maybe also causing mischief).

HONOR NATURE

All goblins are part of nature, so all goblins should respect and honor the nature that they come from. But goblins also know that the definition of nature goes way beyond pretty flowers, rippling brooks, and beautiful landscapes. Nature isn't just a big, beautiful thing—it's all the little nitty-gritty things that come together to make the big, beautiful thing. Nature isn't just wildflowers but also the earthworms and dirt that feed the flowers, the birds and bugs that scatter seeds and pollinate, and the death and decay that are an integral part of the cycle of life. Goblins love every part of nature—particularly the parts that tend to go overlooked.

Being a goblin who loves nature doesn't mean you need to live in the woods and eat nothing but plants. You can be a nature-loving gob who lives in the suburbs, or the big city, or the middle of the desert. Nature is everywhere, no matter where you go, and caring for nature extends beyond inaccessible zero-waste lifestyles. Plant yourself a little windowsill herb garden using empty yogurt containers. Scatter seeds for butterfly-friendly plants in the strips of grass next to the sidewalk. Bring nature into your space by collecting rocks, leaves, flowers, and feathers you find and then displaying them. There are so many ways to invite nature into your life and to care for nature when you can.

SEEK OUT WHAT EMPOWERS YOU

The goblin mindset encourages everyone to make the lifestyle choices that are best suited to their continued happiness and comfort, not the choices that are most approved by the dominant culture. Being a goblin is all about finding what empowers you and building a life around that. A lot of our society is based around public performance, but goblin society is the opposite. Goblins celebrate feeling comfortable in your own body and space. They celebrate ignoring useless social performances in favor of the clothes, decorations, and interests that make you feel most at home.

Ultimately, being a goblin is about creating a weird, grimy little home in a world that prefers to ignore the weird and grimy. Sometimes this can be a scary thing, so you need to arm yourself with your personal comforts and passions to remind yourself that you deserve a place as much as anyone else. Find the things that will make you feel powerful and deserving of space and hold on to them, use them to decorate your nest, and then share them with others to create a network of empowered goblins. Empower yourself and others to make the goblin space in the world a little bigger and a little more inviting.

CHAPTER 2

Turning Over Rocks

How to get in tune with the
ugly parts of nature

There are lots of people who feel like they don't want, or don't need, to engage with nature. Ever. In their entire lives. This could be because they find dirt too dirty, animals too frightening, and bugs just plain gross. However, it's more likely because there's such a large disconnect these days between people and nature. Most of us are never taught how to interact with nature—or even how to find nature in the first place.

Modern people live largely in urban and suburban areas, and in those places it just doesn't seem necessary to know which berry bushes are safe and which are poisonous or how to tell if an animal is angry. This is fair and it makes sense—why learn a bunch of information that you may never need? But it means that when people do have to interact with nature (as we all do at some point, no matter where we live), they approach it with fear, distrust, and ignorance. They don't see nature as a place to find joy and comfort, but rather as something to be feared.

But it doesn't have to be! Nature is all around us, and it can offer us so much. Spending time in nature has been proven to reduce stress and elevate mood, but it also offers us a place to think and exist that doesn't cost money and doesn't expect anything from us. Increasingly, it costs money to go almost anywhere. There are very few places that we can go and not be expected, or forced, to spend money. But going on a walk, going to a park, and even just standing outside are all free. Spending time outside is a radical act of anti-capitalism (which is part of why goblins are all about it).

Going outside also offers us a chance to be curious, to think about the connections between living things, to move our bodies in different ways, to get a close-up view of how the world works. You could sit inside and read a book about ants, or you could go outside and follow some ants around for an hour and see what they're up to and then come back to your book about ants with new eyes. There's so much that we can learn about our world from going outside, and understanding our world can also offer us a better understanding of one another.

Of course, the outdoors are positioned more and more as a playground for rich, white, able-bodied people. We can't talk about nature without talking about lack of access to nature, whether physical or sociological, and general gatekeeping. Probably the last person you saw post about going on a hike was a skinny white celebrity who ran up that "mountain" in LA that skinny white celebrities are always running up.

Wealth offers more access to green spaces, both nearby and far away. Think about how much New York City apartments with a view of Central Park cost. (Central Park, by the way, was built partially on top of a Black neighborhood called Seneca Village.) Wealthy people have greenery right outside their front doors, but they can also afford to travel and see even more nature. Nature must be good for us if the wealthy are hoarding it for themselves.

And if you have any sort of disability or health challenges, it's not always accessible to go to a park or otherwise engage with nature. There aren't often paved pathways on hiking trails, public bathrooms and rest spaces aren't well maintained, and being outside in a large park or natural area means there's a risk of being stranded. We don't always think of nature as something that needs to be made accessible, but of course it should be. It seems obvious that everyone should have access to the outdoors, but we need to work to make outdoor spaces accessible, and that work usually doesn't happen.

So, what do we do if nature is so great but also inaccessible? Well, obviously we steal it back. We're goblins, after all. Nature belongs to the people, and goblins are for the people. Summon all your goblin strength and courage and go for a walk. If you can, visit a park or some other natural area. Take up space! Take your own Instagram photos! Be an anti-capitalist troublemaker! Participate in the radical act of going outside, and encourage your goblin friends to do the same.

If you want to know more about nature and your local ecosystems before heading outside, here are some great ways to expand your natural knowledge:

- The library! Duh! All libraries are goblin-friendly spaces, since they're free institutions dedicated to serving the community and sharing knowledge.

- Check out the organization that oversees public parks in your area—you could visit a nearby office or research them online. They'll likely have lots of information about local parks and ecosystems.

- Visit the websites of local, regional, and national fish and wildlife services. These are great resources for learning about all kinds of local animals and their habitats.

- Visit your local community garden. If there isn't a community garden near you, maybe you could start one. Community gardens are a great way to bring people together in and around green spaces, and they teach tons of useful skills.

- Visit your local botanical garden and ask lots of questions. Botanical gardens are awesome, although they usually aren't free (bummer). But if you can afford to visit, it's a great way to interact with nature in a city in a controlled, educational environment (read: there are lots of cards telling you what the different plants are, and you probably won't get attacked by a bear).

When you visit any of these places, ask the experts questions! Asking experts questions about their area of expertise is honestly a treat for everyone. If you're too anxious to talk to the gardeners or park rangers because you think you're bothering them, consider that you might actually be making their day.

Nature Is Everywhere

Consider: nature. Are you considering it? What images are coming to mind? Probably trees swaying in the breeze, river rocks shimmering under a gently burbling stream, snow-capped mountains turning pink in the evening sun—all the usual Robert Frost slash Walt Whitman slash John Muir splendor that we've categorized as capital-N Nature. This type of nature is wonderful, of course. There's a reason poets love writing about it. However, not everyone has access to wilderness, and even if they do, their wilderness might look nothing like this. (There are seven biomes in the world, after all.)

Capitalism loves to categorize, so it's not surprising that most people have been conditioned to view nature through such a narrow lens. We think "wild animal" only when we're looking at grizzly bears and Dall sheep, not squirrels and rats. We think "the great outdoors" only when we're on top of a mountain, instead of every time we step outside. It's great that there are places in the world that feel as wild and untamed as the poets said they should, but let's imagine that we aren't people who have a national park in our backyard. Let's imagine we've lived our lives somewhere urban or suburban, and the closest we can get to climbing a mountain this afternoon is taking the stairs instead of the elevator to our office. How do we get in touch with nature? Where can we find it? And most importantly: is it free?

Good news, aspiring goblin. Nature is everywhere. This is due to the often-ignored fact that we live on Earth, and Earth is actually made of nature. It's nature all the way down. Everywhere you look, nature. Everywhere you step, nature. Look out your window—do you see the sky? The clouds in the sky? The sun or moon or stars? The birds, maybe sparrows or starlings or geese? All of these things are nature. You yourself are nature; you are made up of nature, you rely on nature for your life, you are in and of nature, you are an important part of the natural world. If you learn to look at the world around you with this point of view, you'll realize that you're much more in touch with the natural world than you thought.

Here's an exercise to practice seeing nature:

1. **Get dressed and step outside your front door.** Make sure you're wearing something comfortable and weather appropriate, something you can move around in.

2. **Go for a walk, but do it slowly.** If you're in a busy city, this might mean you have to stay on the edge of the sidewalk to get out of people's way. (Note that even if you think you're not allowed to walk slowly in your city, it's actually fully legal and other people are doing it all the time. Please also note that I'm using *walk* as a general term, and if you use any kind of mobility aid, you can still participate in this exercise.)

3. **Look around.** Spend some time just looking up at the sky and some time just looking down at the ground. Maybe stop or slow down every time you see a tree or a bush and spend a few seconds thinking about what makes this tree different from the last one you saw. Give yourself time to reflect on what you're looking at, instead of passively taking it in.

4. **Pay attention to plants.** If you're in a city, this might look like checking out those carefully spaced sidewalk trees, or someone's window box of plants a few stories up, or some other planned bit of greenery. If you're in a suburb, this might look like noticing the weeds on someone's lawn, or a tree shedding leaves over the sidewalk, or a neighbor's garden. Wherever you are, there are likely plants nearby, even if the "plants" are just grass. Look at these plants carefully, snap some pictures, take a moment to look up what exactly you're looking at. Find something you like or dislike about the plant. Touch the plant, see what it feels like in your hand. Treat yourself to a moment of interaction with greenery.

5. **Brake for animals.** Pay attention to bugs like ants and flies: Where are they going? What did they land on? Watch a bird or squirrel steal the bagel someone dropped on the sidewalk, watch the subway rat navigate the candy wrappers that have blown onto the train track. Think about why the deer are eating the grass in this yard, instead of the neighbor's. These animals may seem more mundane or commonplace than lions and tigers and bears, but that doesn't mean they interact with the world any less. We're lucky to live in a world with all kinds of animals.

> Leave the damn animals alone! Do not approach them, even
> if they're just squirrels or seagulls. Give all wild animals
> their space. Admire from afar.

6. **Take nothing but pictures (unless you find a cool rock).** Don't take home small animals or important pieces of their local ecosystems, but if you notice a cool rock or leaf, pick that shit up. (Make sure it's not illegal to take rocks or leaves from the area you're in—some parks have laws about taking things with you.) Leaves can be pressed under a stack of books and kept fresh that way, and rocks can be set around your apartment as cute decorations. Just be sure to never take more than 10 percent of what's there!

7. **Take notes.** When you're done with your walk, take some notes about what you saw. You can jot down a few quick reminders of your favorite moments or wax poetic about the way the sun was hitting a spiderweb—there's no wrong way to record your experiences. These notes are nice to turn to in times when you feel distant from nature, and they are a good reminder that nature is never really that far away.

Bringing Nature Home

Did you know that a *manuport* is a natural object that you take from its original location but leave otherwise unchanged? If you pick up a rock when you're out and about and you bring that rock home and put it on your bookshelf without polishing, painting, or otherwise decorating it, you've created a manuport. If you find a piece of quartz, or a clamshell, or a small fossil in your backyard and you send it to a friend as a gift, you've created a manuport (maybe give the clamshell a rinse before you send it though, so your friend doesn't end up with a stinky gift). These little natural objects are simple to make—so simple that they require almost no effort at all. What makes them so special, then?

It turns out that manuports have been around for as long as humanity, and even before we were strictly considered humans, in fact. Plenty of archeological sites have found small natural objects made from minerals or materials that were only available many miles away from the site, meaning that an ancient person found a rock shaped like a face somewhere far from home and carried that rock back with them. Because these historical manuports are often beautiful or striking in some way, they're sometimes considered one of the earliest forms of art. Isn't it remarkable to think that by picking up a cool rock and bringing it to a friend, you're engaging in the most ancient form of art? Isn't it remarkable to think that making art can be as simple as recognizing beauty and choosing to share that beauty with others?

GOBLIN NATURE IN THE DESERT

I know what you're thinking: "This goblin stuff is great, but I live in the desert! Mushrooms and moss are rare in my biome. Can I still be a goblin?" The answer is yes, anyone in any biome can be a goblin. But let's get into why desert biomes are particularly conducive to the goblin lifestyle.

🍄 Instead of **mushrooms**, look for **succulents:** Looking for some weird little guys that grow close to the ground, need very little care, and have a crazy amount of biodiversity? Don't worry, desert goblins, you don't need mushrooms to meet these needs—succulents are the perfect desert substitute for everyone's favorite fungus. They come in all different shapes and sizes, and they're easy to grow inside, so you can keep them in your goblin den.

🍄 Instead of **moss**, look for **brittlebush:** Okay, so moss actually can grow in deserts (because of course it can), but if you're in a desert biome you're a lot more likely to find brittlebush. This little shrub grows everywhere and, bonus, it has really pretty yellow flowers. Like moss, brittlebush is hardy and nice to look at, but it also has a lot of uses. From glue to medicine to varnish and incense, there's little the brittlebush can't do.

🍄 Instead of **toads**, look for **lizards:** Why go slimy when you can go scaly? There are so many cool lizards in the desert, you won't even miss frogs and toads. Plus, lizards are goblin-y as hell. Their body temperature is wack, their scales are weird, and they're a strange mix of cute and upsetting. That's everything a goblin could ask for in a familiar.

> Remember, don't approach wild animals, even if they're small and delicate! Appreciate your lizards from afar and they will appreciate you right back.

🍄 Instead of **earthworms**, look for **scorpions**: Oh, you're interested in some creepy little wiggly thing? Some unearthly squiggly guy? Some weird little fellow who would make decent people everywhere run for the hills? If you can't find a worm, just wait till you hear about scorpions. Scorpions are like if worms put on suits of armor and got so mean, and we love that for them. Like worms, scorpions don't get a lot of love, so do your goblin duty and welcome these little dudes into your goblin hearts.

Don't Forget to Look Down

When's the last time you went outside and spent the whole time looking up? Probably never, because it would be weird—and frankly irresponsible—to walk around looking up all the time. You could get hit by a car or a bike or just be really in the way of other people trying to walk around (which isn't immediately life-threatening but is super annoying). However, there's plenty of people out there who will tell you to look up more. Look up from your shoes, from your phone, from your book, and see what's happening in the world.

What these people don't understand is that there's just as much world happening on the ground as there is anywhere else. Here are just a few of the many, many things that can be found on the ground: bugs (including super cool bugs), dirt, moss, roots, sidewalk cracks, stuff that grows in sidewalk cracks, fungus, and rats and other cool little guys. These ground-bound weirdos are just as interesting as anything you can find in the sky. Why not embrace that? Spend more purposeful time looking down and explore your world that way. Let's dig into some of the cool stuff you'll find when you're looking down instead of up.

Let's talk about bugs. What's going on with those little guys? You've probably heard the (completely untrue) statistic about people swallowing eight spiders per year in their sleep, or the (equally untrue) statistic about how you're never more than ten feet from a spider. It sometimes feels like most of our well-known bug facts are just anti-bug propaganda. But bugs aren't the bad guys! They're actually extremely cool and extremely important to their ecosystems. They're really tiny, small-scale nature that lives in your house—and everywhere else. Here are some bugs that all goblins should know.

MOTHS: Ah, the moth, the butterfly's simple, slightly creepier cousin. You might be familiar with moths as little gray guys who obsessively flock to light, but there's much more to them than that. Here are some lessons we can learn from moths:

- **Allow yourself space to grow.** Just because you've always been a caterpillar, it doesn't mean you'll always stay a caterpillar. If you want to change, create space in your life for change (even if it's only a little space at first). Seek out quiet, look inward, and figure out who you want to become.

- **Seek the light.** You might look at a moth slamming itself against a streetlight and think, "That's embarrassing." But at least that moth knows what it wants. Find the thing that you want, that brings you joy and fuels you, and go for it. Don't let anything get in your way, because you deserve to find your light and stand in it.

SPIDERS: Spiders get a bad rap, which is unfair because they're integral to so many different ecosystems. This is a pro-spider space, and we're here to support and learn more about our little arachnid friends. Some spider lessons:

- **Create a home you love.** People think cobwebs are creepy, but those dainty little webs are actually beautifully built homes. No matter what your living space, find a way to make your home feel like *your* home, even if that just means putting up art that you made or keeping your favorite blanket handy. Having a space where you feel safe and comfortable will improve all the other parts of your life.

- **Contribute to your ecosystem.** Spiders do so much for us and get so little thanks. They're always working to get rid of pests and make the world a better place. Next time you see a spider, instead of freaking out, ask yourself what you could do to make your community a better place and how you could organize to improve the lives of those around you.

WORMS: Worms are some real freaks and we love that for them. These wriggly slimy ooey-gooey weirdos are a goblin's best friend because they encapsulate the goblin lifestyle so well. Here's what worms can teach us:

- **Gender is fake.** Did you know that all earthworms are hermaphroditic? They understand what it's like to have a complicated relationship to gender, but they also know that you never need to have it all figured out. Gender is a performance and it's okay to get weird with it.

- **Don't be afraid to get messy.** Worms spend basically their entire lives in the dirt, just eating and pooping and redistributing nutrients. The worm lifestyle is a good reminder that we could all benefit from spending more time in the dirt, whether that means literally going outside more or embracing the messier parts of ourselves. We're all a little weird and a little grimy, but that doesn't mean we're unworthy of love or space. Take it from the worms: love the dirt you're in.

MOSS

Moss is a simple little plant that contains some truly incredible features. Moss can absorb liquid up to twenty times its weight, needs little to no care in order to grow (and thrive) in almost any environment, and is great at cleaning pollutants out of the air. Ideally, we would all have lawns made of moss instead of grass, but since that's a little larger than the scope of this book, let's talk about how to make a miniature moss garden.

Moss is very hard to kill, and can even come back after extreme dehydration, so this is a great gardening project for goblins who tend to start out with potted plants and end up with pots of dirt. This moss garden can be made almost entirely with materials that can be found around your house or backyard (although if you don't have a backyard, you might have to buy a few extra things).

1. **Decide what size you want your moss garden to be.** It could be as small as a tin of mints or as large as a bucket. You can use anything from a teacup to a ramen bowl to, yes, an actual plant pot as a container for your moss garden. Choose the container that best fits in your space and best represents you.

2. **If your container doesn't have drainage holes in the bottom, put down a layer of pea gravel or other pebbles.** If you want to get fancy, you can drill holes in the bottom of your container, put down a layer of landscaping fabric, and then add pea gravel, but we're generally simple folk who make do with just gravel.

3. **Add about an inch of potting soil.** Spray the potting soil with some water so it's damp, then pack the soil down so it isn't loose. You can also shape the potting soil into little ridges and valleys to add depth to your moss garden.

4. **Place your moss.** Be thoughtful about this, take your time, and be gentle with the moss. Tuck the moss nicely into its container, trim it into the shape you like, and, if you want, mix different mosses together to get interesting color and texture combinations. You can cover all the soil or leave some exposed, trim the moss perfectly into the container or let it hang out a bit. This is your garden, so make sure you're creating something you like.

5. **Water your garden.** Whenever planting or transplanting plants, you want to make sure the plant and soil are good and moist. Don't drown your moss, but make sure both the moss and soil are damp. After you're done making the garden, mist it regularly and water twice a week—again, don't overwater, just make sure it feels moist. If you're not sure if the plant needs water, gently stick a finger in the soil. If the soil is dry, give the garden some water. If it's wet, give it time to dry out.

6. Decorate. You can place small rocks, dried flowers, bark, sea glass, or even little figurines in your garden. Get creative with your decor and have fun with this. Try to make a moss garden that a goblin would be happy to live in.

7. Find a home for your moss garden. Once you're finished with your garden, place it somewhere with bright, indirect sunlight. If you don't have the right light in your living space, you may need to find a plant light or place your garden somewhere outside.

8. Admire it. Take some time to appreciate what you just made. Think about how it looks in your living space with your other things. Think about what you did well when making the garden and what choices you made that led to such a lovely little piece of greenery. Goblins love admiring their things, and a miniature moss garden is sure to give you a lot to admire.

MAKE A MUSHROOM SPORE PRINT

Scientists and mushroom foragers have been using spore prints to cultivate and identify mushrooms for hundreds of years. Spore prints are extremely useful for mushroom enthusiasts, but they also make very cool art, and they're really easy to make. Here's a quick-and-dirty guide to making your own spore print at home.

WHAT YOU'LL NEED

- ★ Paper bag (to hold mushrooms if you're foraging)
- ★ Gloves (for handling the mushrooms)
- ★ Mature mushroom with gills (those thin ridges under the cap that look like pleated fabric or book pages), either foraged or store bought
- ★ Paper
- ★ A glass or jar

WHAT TO DO

1. You can do this project with mushrooms bought from the grocery store, but if you'd like to harvest your own, look for mushrooms after a heavy rain because you'll have better luck. Bring a bag for collecting them, and wear gloves!

2. Cut the mushroom stem off as close to the cap as you can without damaging the gills.

3. Place mushroom cap, gills down, on a piece of paper— no need to press the mushroom down, just place it lightly on the paper. Cover the mushroom with a jar or glass. Leave the container in place for 12–24 hours.

4. Remove the container and gently lift up the mushroom cap. The spores should have dropped and left an imprint of the bottom of the mushroom cap on your paper.

5. That's it, you're done! You now have some great, simple goblin art to decorate your goblin home.

Different types of mushroom have different colored spores, and mushrooms that are fresher or more mature might make more vibrant spore prints than mushrooms that are too young or too old. Experiment with different kinds of mushrooms to get all kinds of prints!

MUSHROOMS AND FUNGUS

There are literally millions of extremely diverse species of fungus, and although you can't always see it, we rely on various types of fungus for almost every aspect of life on earth. From making food to curing diseases, we couldn't do much without fungi. Since fungus is such a broad category, let's focus more specifically on the crown jewel of the mycological world: the mushroom.

Mushrooms are having a real moment lately, which is great because they deserve it. People are finally seeing mushrooms as more than a lumpy-looking health hazard, and they're appreciating the varied aesthetics of these strange plants (although technically fungi are more animal than plant). You may be thinking, "But people view *me* as a lumpy-looking health hazard! Why don't they see the charm of my goblin aesthetic?" This is a fair question, since goblins and mushrooms have so much in common—both are strange, dirty, unkillable, etc. It makes sense that we should learn from each other, and goblins can borrow what they like from mushrooms. So here's a guide to updating your look to be more closely in line with the bizarre beauty of mushrooms.

Keep your aesthetic difficult to nail down. Just as the words *mushroom* and *fungus* are used to describe a huge range of weird animal-plants, so too should your aesthetic be wide-ranging and complex. Don't worry about identifying only as a "plant girl" or an "art ho" or an "old-timey circus clown"—instead of trying to capture your style in simple terms, let it be expansive. Borrow from goths and preps equally, and then add '90s bubblegum pop glitter queen as an accent. Don't worry too much about other people understanding your style, just do your own thing for yourself.

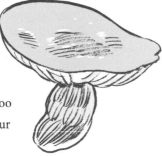

Get a little weird with it. Mushrooms are well-known as psychedelics, so why not embrace the strange in your personal style? If you want to pair some colors that don't normally go together or wear a lot of corsets or dye your hair snot-green, nobody's stopping you. Explore all your eccentric style urges, lean into all your bizarre tastes. It's likely that

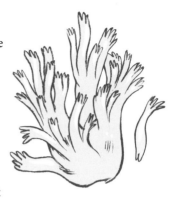

what you find when you're exploring the weirder parts of your style will end up feeling more comfortable and personal than anything you've tried before.

Decay exists as an extant form of style. Mushrooms thrive on things that are old, used, and starting to break down, so why shouldn't you? Get into thrifting and become a part of clothing's natural life cycle. Just as mushrooms help fallen trees become soil, you can help a forgotten pair of corduroys become stylish. Whether this means that you begin haunting local thrift stores to curate your ideal used wardrobe or you decide to alter and update a handful of secondhand dresses so they suit you better, there are all kinds of ways to make existing clothing into something brand-new.

Flourish in the dark. Most of the mushroom life cycle takes place underground, where the fungus takes its time growing and readying itself before emerging into the world. If you're interested in trying a new style but nervous about bringing that style out in public, it's perfectly fine to spend time refining your new look in the comfort of your own space. Embracing your privacy doesn't mean you're ashamed of yourself, it means you're giving yourself time to get comfortable with new parts of your identity without added pressure. Give yourself the space you need to understand who you are outside the public eye. Then, just like a mushroom, you can eventually emerge from the dirt and show off your amazing new look.

Do the most. If you look at pictures of three different kinds of mushrooms, you're likely to see three alien-looking organisms that seemingly have nothing to do with each other. Oyster mushrooms look like seashells growing off the sides of trees, morels look like an army of termites moved into a peach pit, and beech mushrooms all grow together in a fist of tiny mushroom caps. All these different mushrooms are going for it, full bore, no holds barred. They are *not* willing to sacrifice their looks just to become easier to categorize or less weird, and neither should you. If you like something, wear it. If you want to look a certain way, go for it. Why do a little when you can do a lot?

> *Doing the most* just means committing fully to your style. If your personal aesthetic is muted, you don't need to wear bright colors, you just need to embrace more neutrals or whatever it is that feels right to you.

Nature is weird and miraculous and absolutely everywhere—it's a lot like goblins in these ways. If you start thinking of the natural world as a friend, a constant goblin companion who sometimes needs space but is always looking out for you, then suddenly the world seems a lot friendlier. Plants and bugs that might have seemed distant or strange before are suddenly familiar and warm once you realize that you're all part of nature. Go make friends with the dirt! Watch your beetle buds crawl around and take pictures of your mushroom pals. They're all goblins too, after all.

CHAPTER 3

Goblin Finery

Finding and making the comfy
clothes of your dreams

Basically everyone has a weird relationship to clothes. But what if instead of wearing clothes that made you feel hyperaware of society's expectations for your body, you wore clothes that made you feel comfortable and happy? Maybe even clothes that made you feel good, or at least neutral, about how you looked? Yes, this is actually possible to do!

Because goblins are all about comfort, emphasizing personal style, and finding empowerment, dressing in goblin style means wearing clothes that look good to you without worrying about trends, finding clothing items that genuinely feel comfortable on your body, and ensuring that no matter what you choose to wear, your clothes make you feel happy. This chapter might not cure your clothes anxiety, but hopefully it will make you feel more empowered to seek out clothing that makes you feel good. Let's reconsider what it means to be stylish, sustainable, and comfortable when it comes to our clothes.

Rethink Your Relationship to Clothes

When buying clothes, how often do you take into account the way the fabric feels on your body? Every time you try something on, or just when buying clothes for movement? What would your closet look like if you paid more attention to the way your clothes feel instead of how they look? Go to your closet now and try on your three most stylish articles of clothing (at the same time or separately, up to you). Stretch a little in the clothes, sit down in them, go through some of your daily movements in the clothes, but pay special attention to the feel of the fabric on your body. Do any of the clothes have uncomfortable zippers? Are any of them too small? Does the fabric feel scratchy, are the pockets in the right places? Are there any pockets at all?!

After you've tried this little exercise with your cool clothes, try it again with your most comfortable articles of clothing. What differences in feeling do you notice between your favorite clothes and your coziest clothes? Where do you tend to wear your comfortable clothes: around the house or running errands? How does your body feel in the cozy clothes: squished, squeezed, and chafed, or held? How does the way your body feels make *you* feel?

This exercise isn't intended to make you throw away your most stylish clothing, but rather to reconsider what it means to feel good in your clothes. If your definition of feeling good begins and ends with looking good, that's fine, but maybe that definition could be expanded to make more room for your physical comfort. If your definition of feeling good doesn't seem appropriate for leaving your house, reflect on who made the rules about what it means to be presentable, and question how often you really agree with the concept of presentable anyway. What would you dress like if you could wear whatever you wanted, whenever you wanted, and not have to worry about judgment from others? You'd probably be a lot more comfy and your clothes would be a lot more fun. Fashion is complicated, but clothing is created to protect us and our bodies from the world. If your clothes are doing that, they're doing their job.

Slip into Something More Comfortable

Goblins value clothes for their comfort, their durability, their sustainability, and their protection over the ways their clothes conform to whatever style is currently popular. This doesn't mean you can't dress cute; rather, it's an opportunity to rethink what dressing cute means to you. Why wear something

that doesn't feel good on your body and seems inauthentic to your personal style when you could express yourself while also feeling good? Have faith in your fashion sense, even if what you like to wear is outside the norm. Prioritize having a positive experience in your clothes and in your body by wearing pieces that make you feel relaxed and unrestrained.

Goblin clothes tend to be timeless and very comfortable, rather than trendy and uncomfy. Some people might associate this style with sloppiness or feel like it's not professional or presentable. But why do we conflate being comfortable with being unstylish and unattractive? Isn't it actually more attractive to be at ease? At its core, dressing comfortably means dressing in clothes that don't actively cause you pain or annoyance. But dressing comfortably also means wearing clothes that make you feel relaxed and that you don't need to keep thinking about every few minutes because you need to adjust them, or they're hurting you, or you don't really like how you look in them. Comfortable clothes are clothes that put your mind at ease and let you go about your day without added anxiety. Trendy clothes tend to do the opposite of this, since they're all about fitting yourself into a style, rather than finding a style that fits you.

Our clothes are supposed to serve us as we move through our days, but so often we end up dressing to serve others instead of ourselves. Let's flip that idea on its head and start dressing for ourselves. Find clothes that make you feel confident and turn your clothing into a form of self-care. It can feel overwhelming to rethink your relationship to clothes, but remember that you can begin with small things. This exercise will help you slow down as you get dressed and really consider what you want to put on your body. Use this exercise to tune in to your body and listen to yourself and your particular sense of style.

1. Find all your most comfortable clothes and lay them out around you. (Remember that *comfortable* here means clothes that feel good on your body and put your mind at ease—these could be pajamas and sweatpants or a few dresses that fit you just right.)

2. Spend a moment running your hand over your clothes, feeling the texture and thickness of the fabrics. Consider what you like about these textures and how they feel on your body. Think about when you choose to wear these clothes.

3. Close your eyes and try to focus on how your body feels today. Are you cold? Hot? Tired? Do you have pain anywhere? Give yourself time to really tune into how your body is feeling. Maybe even do a body scan meditation (these are easy to find online if you need a guide).

4. Once you're feeling more in touch with your body, think about what your different items of clothing can offer you today. Maybe you woke up sweaty and you want to wear a T-shirt, or your room is cold and you want to wear sweatpants. Maybe your back hurts and you know that wearing comfy tennis shoes all day will help. Take a minute to think

about what your body needs and decide which items of clothing can best serve you today.

5. Get dressed in whatever clothing you chose, but don't force yourself to look in the mirror if you don't want to. You don't need to spend time inspecting your clothes and body before you start your day. Remind yourself that you didn't dress for anyone else today, and frankly it never matters how you appear to others. What matters is that you feel good.

6. If you notice yourself checking your look in a mirror and thinking negative thoughts, close your eyes and try to tune back in to how your body feels. Think about how the clothing you chose is helping your body today and consider how good it feels to dress for yourself and your own comfort. Try another meditation if you need to. You deserve to take time to feel comfortable in your clothes.

7. If after practicing step 6 you still feel uncomfortable in your outfit, feel free to change clothes. Maybe the outfit you chose wasn't working for some reason, and that's okay. We don't always get it in one. You're not being defeated if you can't find comfort in a certain outfit, you're being thoughtful with yourself and aware of your needs.

8. Keep an extra T-shirt or hoodie (or other comfy article of clothing) near you throughout the day, in case you want to change. Our bodies never feel the same all the way through the day, so it's nice to be able to adjust when you need to.

9. At the end of the day, take a moment to consider how you felt in your comfy outfit. Be grateful to yourself for prioritizing your comfort. Be grateful to your pajamas for offering another, new comfort once you take off this outfit. Remember that you did something kind for yourself today, and that's a huge part of being a goblin.

Hopefully after this exercise you feel a little more connected to your clothes and, more importantly, to your body. It can be scary to spend time connecting with your body, and sometimes you find things there that you've been trying to ignore. But if you treat your body well and wrap yourself in comfort, you may find a type of peace that you weren't expecting. Let your clothes be things that increase your peace rather than something distracting. Goblins have way too much stuff going on to worry about itchy tags or painful shoes. Spend a moment listening to the soft animal of your body (shoutout to "Wild Geese" by Mary Oliver) every morning and you'll have more time later in the day to focus on fun goblin tasks, like foraging in the dirt or looking for treasure in the dirt or just sitting in the dirt.

DRESSING COZY IN WARM PLACES

Usually the word *cozy* is associated with warmth, but what do you do if you're a goblin looking to dress cozy in a place where you're always warm? If it's the middle of summer, or if you live in a hot climate, you probably don't want to bundle up in order to get comfy. Luckily, goblins know that coziness is more about feeling good in your clothes than it is about fuzzy blankets and thick sweaters. Here are some ways that goblins in warmer places can get cozy.

🍄 **Cozy means comfy:** The first step to getting cozy is getting comfy, and that means choosing clothes that feel good on you. Think about how your clothes feel on your body. Maybe a pair of denim shorts are nice because they keep you cool, but they always make you feel squeezed and squished when you wear them. Try looking for stretchy shorts or skirts next time you're shopping (or you can even make some yourself!). Give yourself space to consider what actually feels good on your body, and then seek out those types of clothes.

🍄 **Finding fabrics:** Fabrics like linen, cotton, and silk are great for warm weather, because they breathe well and can be thin without being fragile. Plus, they are soft and feel nice to wear. Of course it's not always possible to design your wardrobe around certain fabrics, but if you keep in mind which fabrics feel best on you and in your climate, you can prioritize finding them in the future.

Good shoes, can't lose: Having the right footwear is important no matter the climate, but in sunny places where you're wearing sandals or going barefoot often, it's important to remember what a difference a good pair of shoes can make in your life. Finding a pair of shoes that won't get too hot but also offer proper support can be difficult. If you can't afford fancy shoes, you can still make sure the shoes you buy fit you properly and feel okay on your feet, and finding some good insoles is a cheap but effective way to make your shoes feel better.

Protect your skin: This isn't directly about clothing, but if you live somewhere sunny, don't forget to always wear sunscreen! A smear of sunscreen is the perfect goblin accessory to any warm-weather ensemble.

> If you're allergic to (or just don't like) chemical sunscreens, there are mineral and plant-based sunscreens that work just as well.

Accessories Are a Goblin's Best Friend

If you love clutter, you'll love accessories; they're literally fun clutter that you get to take with you everywhere. Wear your favorite little treasures around your neck or pinned to your lapel, and it'll be like you're taking a piece of home with you everywhere you go. It's like you never really need to leave your home.

Accessories are great for showing the world who you are and what you like. Jewelry, pins, patches, hair ties, belts—all of these allow little pieces of your personality to peek through your outfits. Of course, a goblin is much more than the clothes they wear, but it's nice when your outfits feel like a reflection of at least some parts of you.

Accessories can also allow you to feel seen in new environments or feel comfortable in unfamiliar settings. Jewelry, scarves, and trinkets can lend a surprising amount of ease, even if they're small. Maybe you have a bracelet with homemade charms that remind you of each of your friends or an heirloom ring that's perfect for fiddling with. Accessories like these can make you feel better if you start feeling anxious, or ground you when you're feeling untethered. Here are some fun (and easy) accessories you can make to bring your favorite clutter with you wherever you go.

- **Put a pin in it.** With safety pins and a hot-glue gun, you can make pins out of anything. Bottle caps, googly eyes, pebbles, prizes from a Gashapon machine—use hot glue to affix a safety pin to the back of any small object and you've got a little, meaningful pin.

- **Just add necklace.** Did you know that you can literally string anything onto a chain or cord and have a cool new necklace to wear? Whether you find an old skeleton key at a thrift shop or you happen across a hag stone (a stone with a natural hole in it) by the river or you have an old ring that doesn't fit your fingers anymore, you can pop it on a necklace chain and boom! Instant necklace.

- **Flowers? For accessories? Groundbreaking.** People usually only wear flowers to proms, weddings, and other fancy occasions, but why not wear them every day? Braid some clover into your hair, fill your front overalls pocket with lavender sprigs, put a poppy in your lapel, or just load up your tote bag with a wildflower bouquet. There's no better accessory than a fresh flower. (If flowers aren't currently in season, a silk or paper flower can do the trick too.)

- **Patch things up.** Making your own patches is super easy, and usually very sustainable as well! Just use extra scraps of fabric you have lying around, or cut up clothes you don't like anymore, and use that fabric to make your own patches. You can cut the scraps into fun shapes or draw on them with fabric markers. You could even cut a potato in half, let it dry, and carve a design into it to make your own potato stamp, which would let you print the same design on lots of fabric scraps. Now you and your friends all have cute, sustainable, matching patches!

MAKE A SPECIMEN NECKLACE

Homemade accessories are a staple of goblin finery, and specimen necklaces are about as goblin-y as a home-made accessory can get. Get started on building your collection of goblin accessories by making this specimen necklace.

WHAT YOU'LL NEED

★ Whatever items you'd like to put in your jar: moss, dirt, pebbles, dead bugs, flower petals, crystals, glitter, etc.

★ A small glass jar with a cork stopper

★ Thin wire (18 gauge or higher)

★ Needle-nose pliers or tweezers (or if your jars are particularly tiny, you can use a toothpick instead)

★ Clear glue

★ Necklace chain, cord, or string

★ A jump ring or key ring (optional)

WHAT TO DO

1. First, choose which item(s) you'd like to put in your jar. Glitter, moss, dirt, rocks—it's up to you!

2. Push one end of your wire through the center of your cork stopper. Bend the wire at the base of the stopper so it'll stay hooked in the cork, and turn the wire in a small circle at the top of the stopper to make an eyelet that you can thread your necklace through. Trim excess wire.

3. Use pliers to fill your jar with the items of your choosing. Don't worry about making your items look perfect, because it's going to be almost impossible to perfectly position stuff inside a jar that's the size of your pinkie. Remember that things in jars are usually a little messy! Nobody carefully arranges jam.

4. Apply glue around the outside of the bottom half of your cork stopper. Make sure you get it everywhere the cork will touch the mouth of the jar so the stopper will hold properly. Then insert the stopper into the jar's mouth.

5. Once the glue is dry, thread your necklace chain through the stopper's eyelet. (You could also add a jump ring or key ring to the eyelet and thread the necklace through that.)

6. You're done! You now have a beautiful goblin accessory that's perfect for carrying around your tiniest treasures.

Tips for Thrifting

Looking for clothes can be frustrating: you want something well-made but affordable, something that fits but isn't terrible for the environment. Thrift stores can offer an answer to many of these problems—at an affordable price, even. When you thrift, you're actually doing a great thing for the environment. The fashion industry produces tons of waste, so choosing to buy clothes that have already been worn and loved is a great way to counteract that waste. You're giving clothing a new life when you buy from or donate to a thrift store. Rather than ending up in a landfill, the clothing you buy from a thrift store ends up in your closet. It's literally recycling, but make it fashion.

In addition to being super sustainable, thrift stores are also full of good, cheap clothes. Since everything in the thrift store has been worn before (often many, many times), the clothes are likely durable. Since anyone can donate to a thrift store, you're also getting a huge range of styles (and hopefully a huge range of sizes as well). Obviously the thrift store won't have everything you're looking for every time you go in, but if you broaden your expectations and keep an open mind, you'll be pleasantly surprised at what you find. The better you get at thrifting, the more likely you are to find something you love. Here are some tips to improve your thrifting game.

Sell or donate before you buy. Before you head to the store, do a quick sweep of your closet and pull out some items you don't wear often. Bring these items with you to the thrift store to either sell or donate, and you'll be starting out your thrift journey with a little less stuff in your closet and maybe a little extra money. Some thrift stores will also give you coupons for donating, so there's no reason not to try this!

Set goals for yourself before you go. Thrift stores are the types of places that can easily suck you in for hours, and even though most things are cheap, you might end up leaving four hours later with one hundred dollars worth of colored glass or ceramic picture frames. Sometimes it's fun to waste a day in a thrift store, but if you're on a mission, it's useful to set some goals before you leave the house. You could set a budget for yourself, make a list of clothes you need, limit yourself to a few sections of the store per visit, or set a timer so you can only be in the store for an hour. Whatever type of limit your brain responds to best is what you should use.

Dress for thrifting success. Not all thrift stores have changing rooms, so it's good to dress in clothes that you can easily slip other clothes over. Wearing leggings or bike shorts with a close-fitting shirt will make it much easier for you to try on your finds the second you see something you like, regardless of whether there's a changing room.

To check if a pair of pants will fit before you try them on, hold the pants with one side seam to your belly button and the other wrapped around to your back. If one side seam can touch your belly button while the other seam touches your spine, the pants should fit! This also works with skirts and dresses.

Inspect the quality and condition of the clothes you find. When you find items that you like, take a moment to check that there aren't any stains, holes, worn-out areas, or anything else that might end up being more trouble than the clothes are worth. Turn clothes inside out to check for wear, and feel the fabric to find out if it's too scratchy or covered in pills. (Pills are the little clumps of thread and lint that build up on fabric over time.) Also, take a second to look at the labels. Checking the label informs you about fabrics and brands and where the clothes were made, which is all great information to have. As all goblins know, thrift stores often sell nice items at a low price. Checking the label can ensure that you're getting clothes that will last a long time, in addition to guaranteeing that you're finding some good treasure.

Take a time-out to go through the clothes you picked. It's easy to overshop, especially at a thrift store where you can get an armload of clothes for a few dollars. Every time you rack up more than five items, pause and look through them. Ask yourself if the fabric is actually as soft as you want, if the fit feels comfortable. Maybe think about what clothes you already own that you'd wear with your new picks or which clothes you already own that are too similar. Do you like that dress because it's your style or because it's three dollars? Can you really picture yourself wearing those boots? Taking a time-out to reassess your purchases is a great way to make sure you'll love your wardrobe.

> Try to put unwanted clothes back in a way that doesn't cause extra trouble for the staff, if you can.

Know when to shop. Thrifting is best done during the week rather than on the weekend. If you're an intense thrifter, you might even consider asking staff what days of the week they put out new items and then shopping on those days. It's also a great idea to shop the off-season at thrift stores. This means shopping for winter jackets in summer and sundresses in colder months. You're way more likely to find a good deal when the clothes you're looking for aren't in season. Unlike regular stores, which tend to rotate their stock based on season, thrift stores usually have clothes from every season available year-round. This is great for goblins who like to think ahead and find good deals or goblins who always get hot in the winter or cold in the summer.

With these tips, any goblin should be able to enter a thrift store with confidence and leave with some wardrobe staples. Thrift stores are like treasure hunts, and even though it can take a few trips to find what you're looking for, you'll be glad you put in the time once you find your treasure. Getting clothes that are comfortable and well-made at a low price is a great feeling, and it's great for both your wallet and the environment. Every goblin deserves to have clothes that will serve them well and feel good to wear. Thrift stores are a wonderful place for anyone looking to goblin up their wardrobe.

A DECADENT GOBLIN'S GUIDE TO THRIFTING

Listen, goblins come in all types. Some want to know the quickest way in and out of a thrift store, and some prefer to spend a full day walking up and down every aisle, looking at every article of clothing and digging through bins. If you're the type of goblin who wants to luxuriate in a thrift shopping day, we have some thrifting tips for you too.

🍄 **Clear your schedule.** Don't visit the thrift store on a day when you only have an hour to spare. Give yourself a full day to wander around and look at every little thing. Make thrift shopping feel like a luxurious form of self-care by blocking out special time for it. Even if you're only looking for one or two things, giving yourself time to look around is going to feel a lot better than a desperate thirty-minute search. Thrifting can be tough, so give yourself time.

🍄 **Look at everything.** Maybe you came in looking for pants and you weren't even going to glance at the housewares section. Why limit yourself? Sit on all the furniture, even if you aren't looking for furniture. Go through the men's T-shirt aisle twice, look at the prom dresses, spend time checking out the glassware. If you're looking for treasure, you're likely to find some in unexpected places.

Treat yourself. If you have a few extra dollars to spare, budget those toward the unexpected. Put aside five dollars whenever you visit the thrift store to spend on something you weren't looking for when you came in. This gives you wiggle room if you find something really cool, but helps prevent overspending. It's still a treat even if it's a small treat!

Switch up your routine. If you always shop for shirts in the women's section, try spending a thrift trip looking through the men's shirts instead. (Gendered clothing is a fake idea anyway.) If you always start in the sweater section, try looking in blazers first. Visit the store on different days of the week and at different times so you can find the time that you like best. Try going in with a list if you usually go without, or vice versa. Changing your routine is going to help you figure out what works best for you and your particular goblin brain.

Bring a friend. Everything's better with a friend and thrifting is no exception. Two pairs of eyes looking around the store is way more likely to bring in great goblin treasures, and you have someone to give you feedback on your potential purchases so you don't have to do all the decision-making yourself. Plus it's just nice to spend time with friends! Thrifting together is a great way to make time for being social while also crossing items off your to-do list.

Organizing a Goblin Clothing Swap

Maybe you and your friends are short on money but long on clothes you don't wear anymore. If you don't like thrift shopping or can't go for any reason, bring the thrift store to you by organizing a clothing swap with some friends. A clothing swap is like a party where everyone brings clothes they were going to donate and then you shop for free from one another's closets. You can organize a swap with a big group of people or just a few friends. It's a great way to find new clothes you might not have picked up on your own, and goblins are all about finding new and interesting treasures.

Clothing swaps are goblin-friendly for a ton of reasons. First of all, you get to gather friends and create a community. What is a goblin without a community of other goblins? Why be a single goblin when you could be part of a whole goblin army dedicated to spreading the good goblin word? Clothing swaps are also super sustainable. Instead of buying brand-new clothes, you're shopping secondhand, which is much better for the environment. Clothing swaps are also more likely to be filled with great treasures and cool finds than the average thrift store, since you get to curate your own guest list and you probably have a sense of what your friends like to wear. Best of all, clothing swaps don't involve spending any money. That's anti-capitalism in action, baby!

Clothing swaps are no harder to organize than an average potluck, but here are some tips that'll ensure your friends have a great time at your clothing swap (which is definitely soon to be a celebrated tradition).

Invite a diverse group of friends. If you have one friend who prefers to crochet all their own clothes and another friend who's been strictly goth for the last ten years, you're going to have a lot more fun—and find a lot more treasures—at a clothing swap than if all your friends have the same taste. You don't want to be looking at your friends' clothes and thinking, "I have that same shirt" five or ten times in a row. Imagine what kinds of cool clothes, shoes, and accessories you'll find if you invite your artsy friends *and* your emo friends *and* your granola friends. Now that sounds like a goblin party.

Plan the clothing swap like a party. Have some fun with your swap! Maybe all your friends could bring a snack, or you could draw up your own invitations, make a special playlist, or decorate your space with paper chains and balloons or other cheap, easy decor. Make your swap feel like a special event, and everyone is sure to have a great time. If your friends can tell that you put a lot of effort into your swap, they're sure to put more effort into what they bring. You get out what you put in, so why not put in the plans for a really fun evening with friends?

Think inclusivity. It's going to be a bummer if you invite five friends who wear the same size and one friend who doesn't. Of course, friend groups encompass all shapes and sizes so nobody is going to perfectly fit into everyone else's clothes, but it's good to think about who you're inviting and what you're asking them to bring before you send invites. If your friend group is somehow all one size with a single outlier (seems unlikely, but not technically impossible), you could always host a jewelry and accessories swap to make sure everyone feels included. Being a good goblin means being thoughtful and mindful of others, especially your friends.

Sort out the details ahead of time. To make sure everyone has a great time at your goblin clothing swap, try to be thoughtful and specific with details. Instead of telling your friends to just bring whatever clothes they were going to throw out, make sure you specify that the clothes they bring should be in good condition and (ideally) cute or interesting. Also, be sure to decide how many pieces of clothes everyone should bring. If one person shows up with thirty items of clothing and another person shows up with two, the swap vibes are going to be weird. Tell everyone to bring five items of clothing, or five to ten items. Pick a number or range that seems reasonable and achievable.

Think theme. Of course, you can always throw a general clothing swap. But isn't everything better with a theme? Your theme could be a specific clothing item, like telling guests to only bring dresses or hats or graphic tees. You could also choose a theme like earth tones, or sparkly, or even goblincore, and see what kinds of clothes your friends forgot in their closets that are about to become your new outfit staple. Of course, sometimes it can be hard to find clothes that fit a specific theme, so if you're going that route, it's good to stick to something a little vague or something that your guests can interpret in their own way. You could also set a low limit on the amount of clothes guests are expected to bring or consult on a theme with your friends to find something that works for everyone. Remember, goblins love community and working together.

Patching, Mending, and Upcycling

If you're feeling stoked on upgrading your clothing, improving your sustainability, and highlighting your personal style, you'll love learning about patching, mending, and upcycling. These skills will make your clothing last longer, fit better, and maybe even look cuter! Being able to repair your clothes when they wear and tear will allow you to not only keep and continue wearing great clothes that you might have otherwise gotten rid of, but also add some personal flair to your clothing.

The amount of skill required to sew a patch on a jacket or reapply a button to a shirt or even darn a small hole is relatively minimal. Even someone who's never held a sewing needle could pick up the basics with just a bit of practice. But even though the basics are . . . basic, they can still make a big difference in your life. Knowing skills like sewing and mending will allow you to have a more sustainable wardrobe. It'll also make your life easier: if you lose a button from your favorite jacket, you don't have to worry about who you should ask to sew it back on, whether you should just leave the button off, whether you should give the jacket away, etc. Instead, you can confidently pull out your own personal needle and thread and pop the button back on in just a few minutes. Think about how much time, energy, and stress you just saved with two simple tools.

Mending your own clothes also allows a lot of room for customization and upcycling. Maybe you bought an old jean jacket and you want to cover it in patches, or you want to replace all the brown buttons on a cardigan with green ones. Maybe you have some clothes that could fit a little better. Learning the basics of sewing is going to let you get more creative with your clothes and become even more familiar with what your personal style really looks like. Today you're just learning how to darn a sock, but eventually you could be making your own clothes. But let's not get ahead of ourselves; we should start with the basics.

THREADING A NEEDLE

Let's start all the way at the beginning, because this book is for goblins of every skill level. Before you start sewing, you'll have to thread a needle, which isn't too complicated, but it's worth a quick tutorial. If you struggle with fine motor skills or eyesight, it might be helpful to use a needle threader to make the task easier. Needle threaders are easy to find at craft or big-box stores and usually come with packs of needles.

1. Pull one end of the thread through the eye of the needle. It's best to thread the needle while the thread is still on the spool, instead of cutting off a piece and threading from the cut end, as it keeps the thread grain in the right direction. Thread is made from twisted fibers, and threading against the grain means you're working against that twist, which can make it harder to thread the needle and also make your thread more likely to snarl.

A lot of people will tell you to lick your thread in order to pull it through the eye of the needle more easily, but this is actually bad advice! Licking the thread will cause it to expand when it dries, and it'll become weaker and catch on the rest of your thread as you sew. Instead, cut the thread at a slight angle to give yourself a point to thread with.

2. Unspool about 2.5 times as much thread as you think you need. Pull the needle along the thread until it rests about halfway between the cut end and the spool.

3. Tie the ends of your thread with an overhand knot: Line up the end of your thread with the spool, so you have a loop of thread in one hand and the end and spool in the other hand. Bend your loop toward your other hand, which will create a new loop using both the parallel threads. Pull your original loop through the new loop and pull tight to make a knot.

4. You just threaded a needle. Congratulations! (You can cut the thread now.)

SEWING A BUTTON

Sewing a button is a simple but incredibly useful sewing skill and a great place to start. If you're the kind of person who gets stressed about the implications of that extra button that comes with most store-bought clothes, this tutorial is for you. We're going to learn how to sew a two-hole button, but all buttons will essentially take this same approach.

1. Pick your button and your thread color. If you want the button and thread to match what's already on your clothes, go for it. If you lost a small black button and want to replace it with a big green one, go for it.

2. Thread your needle, but to make the thread thicker and more secure, fold your length of thread in half *before* pulling it through the needle. You might need a needle with a slightly larger eye to do this. Take both ends of the thread and put them both through the eye of the needle, then pull the needle to the thread's halfway point. Fold the thread and tie the two folded ends to each other. This creates a quadruple thread, and it'll help your button stay on better.

3. Find the place where the button used to be on your garment. Poke your needle through the inside of the garment to the outside at a 90-degree angle, and pull the needle until the knot at the end of the thread hits the fabric.

4. Thread your needle through one of the holes of your button. Hold your button on your garment right where you want it to sit, and then push your needle through the button's other hole and through the fabric of your garment. Make sure to pull your thread tight.

5. Continue pushing the needle up through the fabric and the first button hole and down through the second button hole and the fabric. Repeat this process about three times, or until you feel like the button is secure.

6. Loosen your button slightly so it pulls just a bit away from the fabric. Bring your needle up through the back of the fabric to the front, between the fabric and the button (don't pull it through one of the button holes). Wrap your thread around the stitches about ten times to create a thread shank. This keeps your button from being too tight against the fabric to comfortably sit in a button hole.

7. Bring your needle down through the fabric for the last time. Tie a knot in the thread. Make sure the knot is as close to the fabric as possible, and not far down the thread. Cut the thread close to the knot you just tied, and you're done!

SIMPLE HEMMING

Hemming is an easy way to make an article of clothing a little shorter. If you have a skirt that lands at the bottom of your knee instead of the top, for example, you could hem the skirt to make it land where you'd like. Hemming is great because it'll let you adjust the fit of your clothes, or change the style slightly. It's easy and it can help you quickly turn clothes you like into clothes you love, thus keeping more of your outfits in rotation. This tutorial is just going to be the basics of hemming, but it's easy to find more in-depth guides in sewing books or online if you want to get more involved. Also, for simplicity's sake, this tutorial will be about hemming a skirt or dress, although this method can also easily be applied to trousers or loose shirts. (For trousers, you can simply imagine two skirts.)

1. Try on your skirt or dress in front of a mirror so you can tell what length you'd like the skirt to be. Pin the skirt to the length you want. Make sure you insert your pins perpendicular to the hem.
Don't be hasty about this step—really take your time to find a length that feels best to you.

2. Take off the garment and continue to pin the fabric to your desired length around the circumference of the skirt, folding the excess fabric to the inside of the garment. You can put the garment back on to check if it's even, or measure the length of excess fabric you're pin-

ning, or compare your skirt to another skirt in your closet that has the length you're looking for. Pins are usually inserted every 6 inches, but use as many as you need. There's a lot of ways to get the right length and make sure your hem will be even, and you really want your hem to be even. The more even your hem is, the neater your finished product will look.

3. Leave the pins in the skirt and iron the garment around the hem you've created so that you get a crease in the fabric where you'd like your new hem to be. If you're using pins with plastic heads, be careful not to iron the heads! They'll melt and ruin your garment.

4. If you're shortening your skirt considerably, you'll have to trim the extra fabric. Make a mark about 1½ to 2 inches below your crease and cut the excess fabric. Of course, you could just cut your garment to the length you want and then wear it like that, but hemming ensures that your clothes will last longer, since it makes the fabric a little stronger and more resistant to fraying and unraveling.

5. Thread your needle (you can use either of the methods on pages 76–77) with about 2 feet of thread, ideally a color of thread that matches your garment. There are a lot of different stitches you can use to make a hem, but we'll use a straight stitch, since it's pretty simple.

6. Insert your needle into the garment from inside, poking straight through both layers of fabric, about ¼ inch to ½ inch above the crease. Move your needle ¼ inch to the right and insert it straight into the garment from the outside, poking through both layers of fabric. Repeat this process of sending the needle in and out of the garment until your stitches wrap around the length of the garment. For a cleaner finish, make sure to keep the length of the stitches and their distance from the hem consistent all the way around.

7. Once you've stitched all the way around your skirt, just tie off your thread and you're done! This process can also be used to fix a hem that needs mending, if you don't want to create a whole new hemline. And again, there are lots of different stitches you can use to do this, some of which are less visible. Try out a few and see which one makes the most sense to you!

SEWING ON A PATCH

Whether you tore a hole in your favorite pair of jeans or you just want to adorn a jacket or tote bag with some personal flair, knowing how to sew a patch onto your clothes is a great goblin skill to have. Patches can keep your clothes performing even if they get some holes and they let you add a dash of your personal style to a mending job. As a bonus, sewing on patches is really easy to do, and patches are easy to find. If you want cheaper patches, thrift and vintage stores are likely to have a selection of patches for under a dollar or two, or you can make your own patch by cutting material from clothing you don't wear anymore. Patches can be a little expensive if you want a lot of them, and making your own patches from pieces of clothes you don't wear anymore is a great way to save both money and your clothes. (Try painting them with fabric paint before sewing them on!)

1. Choose a patch and figure out where you want it to go. If you're adding a patch for purely decorative reasons, take your time picking a spot where you think the patch looks best. If you're applying a patch for a mending

job, make sure the patch is correctly sized and placed to completely cover the problem area.

2. Once you've chosen a location, use a small piece of double-sided tape or a few pins to hold your patch in place while you sew.

> If you have an iron-on patch, you'll still want to sew it onto your garment. Feel free to iron it on to keep the patch in place while you sew, but sewing the patch will make it much less likely to fall off.

3. Thread your needle.

4. Bring your needle up through the edge of the patch from the inside of the garment to the outside. Pull the thread until the knot at the end of the thread is tight against the fabric.

5. Bring the needle back into the garment through only the garment's fabric. This time you don't want the needle to go through the patch, but you still want to keep your needle as close to the fabric as you can to keep your stitches small.

6. Move your needle over about ¼ inch and bring it back up through the fabric and the edge of your patch, and then down through the fabric near the patch. Repeat this process until the entire patch is sewn down.

7. Tie a knot in your thread once you're finished to hold everything in place, and you're done!

More Ideas for Upcycling

These sewing tips and tutorials will get you started on revamping old clothes, but of course there's so much a creative goblin can do with their old clothes and a few simple craft materials. Upcycling is a fun way to make your clothes feel newer and more personal without spending money on a whole new wardrobe. The goblin life is about rethinking what's right in front of you, and goblins of all skill levels will find a great project among these ideas.

FOR DETAIL-ORIENTED GOBLINS: Try embroidery. Embroidery is a beautiful and cost-effective way to add some charm to any piece of clothing. You can embroider something simple, like a small handful of hearts or flowers, or a more experienced embroiderer could fully cover a shirt in beautiful, threaded designs. Embroidery is a wonderful skill for goblins who like to extrapolate huge beauty from little things.

FOR GOBLINS WHO FIND BEAUTY IN MESSINESS: Try visible mending. This is a technique in which you choose to draw attention to the places where you've covered holes or stains in your clothing. Choose thread that's colored differently from your garment, and draw a simple shape over the area you want to mend, like a heart or a leaf. Use long, vertical stitches to cover the shape, then turn your needle 90 degrees and weave through them. Now you have a cute reminder of your garment's history and your own skill with a needle and thread.

FOR GOBLINS WHO DON'T BELIEVE IN MISTAKES: Try painting. Using fabric paint is a fun and easy way to update your clothes and add fun pops of color. Paint the back pockets of all your jeans, decorate your own tote bags, or make T-shirts for all your goblin friends. If you make a mistake while you're painting, you can just paint over it (and as every goblin knows, there's really no such thing as a mistake anyway). Whether you like small details or large graphics, painting clothes is a great way for every goblin to express themself and make their clothing feel fun and personal.

FOR GOBLINS WHO LIKE TO SHAPE-SHIFT: Try repurposing. If you have an item of clothing that's truly beyond saving, consider what else it could be used for. A moth-eaten old dress might not work as a dress anymore, but it could be cut up and made into kitchen towels or cleaning rags. A pair of jeans with too many holes could be cut up and used to patch up other clothes. A stained T-shirt can be turned into a bag with a little work. Or you could pull the lace off an old skirt and use it in a new sewing project. When you see a garment that's outlived its use as a garment, get creative and consider what other uses it might have. We live in a single-use society, but most of the things we own can actually be reused. Fight the capitalist mindset and reimagine what it means to recycle.

FOR GOBLINS WHO KNOW EXACTLY WHAT THEY WANT: Try reshaping. If you have a dress that's too long or a shirt that's too baggy, break out your needle and thread (or sewing machine) and make your clothes fit exactly how you want. It's amazing how much changing just the hemline or neckline of a piece of clothing can make it feel completely new. Instead of investing in a new wardrobe, try taking in or letting out the sides of a shirt you never wear. Reshaping takes a little more sewing skill but for goblins who love to sew or for goblins who are learning how to sew but aren't quite experienced enough to make their own clothes, this is a great project.

FOR GOBLINS WHO LOVE BUTTONS: Try buttons! Consider this permission to go button-crazy on your clothes. Cover a sweater in buttons, use a different button for each buttonhole of a cardigan, put novelty buttons on a starchy work shirt. The more buttons, the better. The more fun the buttons, the better. If you love buttons, why not embrace that? (Also, don't we all love buttons? A world with more buttons is a better world. Thank you for your service, button-loving goblins.)

FOR GOBLINS WHO LIKE TO WEAR THEIR ART ON THEIR SLEEVE: Try making your own patches. This could be as simple as cutting a colorful old garment into pieces and using those to patch your clothes, or you could do a little more and use a permanent marker or a stamp and fabric paint to print a design on some fabric bits and use those as patches. This is a great way to wear your own art all over your body, like cool fabric tattoos. You could even make patches for your friends so everyone can show off their goblin pride.

Cultivating a good relationship with your clothes is a life's worth of work, but hopefully now you have some tools to get you started on your journey. No one is defined by their clothing, but it's nice to feel like yourself when you get dressed. Rather than prioritizing how other people feel about your clothes, think about how your clothes are serving you, what different pieces can offer you, and how to best showcase your wonderful, unique style every day. Spending time with your clothing is spending time with yourself, and you deserve to spend lots of time on yourself!

NEEDLE-FELT A MUSHROOM PATCH

Now that you're an expert at mending your own clothes, why not have a little fun with it? Follow this tutorial to learn how to use a specialized needle and loose roving to securely and cutely patch holes in wool sweaters (or any wool clothing). This tutorial combines two things goblins love: mushrooms and self-sufficiency.

WHAT YOU'LL NEED

★ Wool roving in two colors, one for the cap and one for the spots (roving is loose wool that hasn't been spun into yarn)

★ A felting sponge, a piece of soft foam, or a regular sponge with a piece of felt over the top

★ Felting needle (these are different from sewing needles because they have barbs on the end that cause the wool to felt)

WHAT TO DO

1. Pick which color of wool you'd like to use for the mushroom cap.

2. Pull off a chunk of your chosen color of wool about twice the size of your hole, roll it into a loose ball, and place it over the hole on the outside of your sweater. Place your foam on the opposite side of the hole on the inside of your sweater.

3. Use your needle to repeatedly stab your wool until you feel the texture of the wool become solid, and you're confident the wool is well-attached to the sweater. Add more wool if you need to. To keep it round, run your needle lightly around the wool as you poke to shape the wool and draw in any loose threads.

4. Take the second color of wool and tear off some small pieces about twice the size you want your mushroom spots to be. Roll each into a loose ball.

5. One at a time, place the spots on the cap and poke them into the cap with your needle. Make sure you place the spots on the outside of the sweater. Round them the same way as you did the cap.

6. Once your spots feel securely felted to your cap, you're done! Now you've got a little extra goblin glamour.

CHAPTER 4

Adorn Your Lair

How to make your living
space goblin-cozy

If you want to turn a house into a goblin home, you've come to the right place. Whether you live in a studio apartment, a dorm room, a house, or a little hut you built in the woods, there are lots of great ways to bring goblin style into your living place. (Although if you're already living in a hut in the woods, you probably don't need advice on how to live a goblin life.) All it takes is a bit of consideration about how you want your space to make you feel.

No matter where you live, you want your place to feel safe and welcoming. But what actually makes you feel safe and welcomed? Try to pinpoint the areas in your house or apartment where you feel the best. Maybe you're really proud of the gallery wall of bug drawings that you organized above your desk, or you love taking a shower because of the eucalyptus stems you hung from your showerhead. It doesn't need to be a big area, but there's probably somewhere in your lair where you prefer spending time. Start being more conscious about these places and you'll begin to piece together what it is that makes you like them so much.

Once you have a better idea of how you want your habitat to make you feel, you can begin bringing these elements into other parts of your space. Fill your apartment with bug decorations! Put plants on every surface! This is your space, and even if your space only extends to your bedroom door, it's just for you and it should make you feel however you want to feel. This chapter will give you lots of ideas on how to cultivate the perfect goblin lair—which is to say, the perfect place for you. From decor to cleaning to incorporating smells and sounds into your daily life, you'll find lots of tips here on how to goblinify your living space.

Clutter? I Definitely Know Her

Some people hear the word *mess* and want to run the other way. But goblins know that every pile of clutter has a warm, dark, cozy center. There's nowhere more comfortable than directly in the middle of all the things you love most. Goblin home decor is all about putting your stuff on display, making your space as cozy as possible, and creating room for your personality. Adorning your lair doesn't mean hiding your taste behind socially acceptable throw pillows and decorating in a way that will impress others. It means putting your tastes on display, all of them, all the time, even if they're a little weird or macabre or gooey. What's going to make you feel better than being surrounded by the things you love that you worked hard to curate?

Let's walk through some of the basic steps to creating an ideal goblin nest.

If you've got it, flaunt it. How many cool items do you have hidden away in drawers and boxes? Probably a lot. You might think the world's not ready to see your collection of raccoon skulls, but cultivating your space isn't about deciding what the world is or isn't ready for. Put all your warped amateur pottery around your TV. String seashells and beach glass from fishing line and hang it in front of a window. Fill jars with loose beads or leaves or twenty-sided dice and display them all around your space. Thinking of fun, clever ways to show off your favorite items is a great way to decorate your lair. Keeping your favorite treasures on display is a constant reminder that the things you love deserve to be seen and admired.

Cozy up. By now you've hopefully gotten the hint that being a goblin involves a lot of cozification. Nowhere is safe from the goblin need to make every surface soft, comfy, and accessible—your space is no exception. Making your nest comfy can mean finding, making, or buying pillows and blankets to place everywhere. It could mean always keeping a hoodie in an area where you like to hang out, just in case you get cold. Making a space that feels cozy is going to look different to everyone, but it's generally going to feel like your space is welcoming you into an embrace rather than hurrying you out the door.

Be yourself. Your lair is your own, and it doesn't need to be decorated in a way that's going to appeal to everyone. There's no point in making your corner of the world work better for someone else than it does for you. Obviously if you live with others, it's important to respect their rules and tastes. But whatever space you can claim as your own is safe to truly make over to your personal taste. Who should your space reflect: the tastes of your favorite influencer who will never see your room, or you, the person who spends lots of time there? Don't tailor your lair to the expectations of others; indulge yourself and maybe even get a little weird with it. Let your personality feel apparent in your space.

What to Collect When You're Collecting

There are few things more satisfying than having a space full of things you love. Collecting special objects and treasures is a staple in goblin culture because it's a great way to physically hold on to memories, interests, and tastes, and even show those things off to other people. Being surrounded by things you love can help remind you of who you are and who you want to be. Goblin collections aren't materialism for materialism's sake, but rather a thoughtful and purposeful curation of beautiful, meaningful things.

Of course, beautiful and meaningful are in the eye of the beholder. Maybe you have a drawer full of paper swans made from sugar packets or you have dried flowers hanging all over your walls. The things you collect don't have to fit a traditional idea of beauty, they just have to be beautiful to you. Your collection also doesn't need to cost you any money—it just needs to feel valuable to you.

Putting together a goblin collection is a great time to rethink the idea of value altogether. The pile of old grocery lists that you keep on your desk might not be worth anything, but it could bring you joy to look at them and remember what they mean to you. A box full of battered birthday cards doesn't need to have a huge resale value to be important to you. It's not bad to care about your things—loving the hoard of beetle exoskeletons you've been curating doesn't make you shallow or materialistic. It makes sense that you'd care a lot about these things you've been thinking about and taking care of and collecting for years! Other people might not value your cool bug shells in the same way, but that doesn't mean they're valueless. The value you place on your objects matters. The way you care for your things is important.

Displaying your collections is a great way to decorate your home, show off the things you love, and make your space feel more personal. Showing off your collections can also be a great way to build community. If you share your collections with friends, both in real life and online, you're telling them about your tastes, values, and interests. By showing people the things that matter to you, you're creating room for people to get to know you better. Maybe you love traveling and you collect cool rocks from every new place you visit, so not only do you have a collection of cool rocks, but also each one is connected to a meaningful memory and experience. Maybe you love corvids and you have a vase in your room filled with crow feathers you've found on the ground as a reminder that your favorite animal is never far away. Collecting isn't about hoarding and materialism, it's about care and celebration and self-expression.

Display Away

Now that you're feeling more confident about displaying your collections, it's time to think about how you can best incorporate the things you love into your decor. Haphazardly dropping every mitten you've ever crocheted on your floor might be an easy way to get your collection out there, but it wouldn't be pleasing or convenient. The difference between a true mess and a happily cluttered goblin nest is intention. Rather than just dumping things everywhere, think about where your items can best serve you and the space. What do you want to feel as you fall asleep at night? What decorations can you put around your bed that will invite that feeling? Put thought into what you bring into every corner of your space, and you'll soon have a cozy nest that any goblin would be happy to live in.

JARS, JARS, JARS!: The great thing about jars is that they come in a ton of different sizes, and basically everything looks good in them. Jars convey a balance between cluttered and contained, and they let you see everything you put inside them. Even better, they're cheap and available basically everywhere. Find some jars of varying sizes and fill each one with a different collection: pens, skipping stones, buttons, rings. Then place your jars anywhere that feels best. They'll look good everywhere, and they allow easy access if you need something inside one of them. Keep a few empty jars hidden away in case you end up with a pile of cords or hair ties that you don't know what to do with. Pop them in a jar and suddenly you have both decor and organization!

BE SHELF-ISH: Storage space and display space are usually kept separate, but shelves are here to bridge that gap and remind you that it's easy to turn your storage into something worth displaying. Shelves are easy to spruce up and personalize, even if you start with ones that look boring. If you get a plain set of shelves at a big-box store, you can paint them the same color as your walls to make your collection of frog figurines stand out. If you find an old bookshelf on the side of the road, you can paint mushrooms on the sides or glue fake flowers to it or line the inside with wallpaper or contact paper. And once your shelves are feeling more personalized, you get to spend time choosing which of your treasures will look best on each shelf. Get creative with what

you display, and consider putting out things that you'd normally keep in a cabinet or closet. Decorating your shelves is an opportunity to rethink which of your treasures you want to see every day.

KEEP IT UNDER GLASS: Shadow boxes are a great way to display things that you wouldn't typically be able to hang on your wall. A shadow box is a shallow box with a glass panel on the front that you can hang on your wall or place on a table. Filling a shadow box with treasures like seashells or rocks or buttons is a fun way to show off a collection, or you could pin or glue items to the backdrop of the shadow box to display anything from vintage clothes to dried flowers to butterflies. Although shadow boxes are much easier to buy than to make, you can also create a quick-and-dirty shadow box by decorating a shoe box (or any box) and hanging that from your wall instead. Shadow boxes elevate whatever you put in them and they're a fun way to give your mundane-seeming treasures a luxurious boost.

CLUTTER, BUT MAKE IT CLASSY: Gallery walls are an extremely goblin-friendly way to decorate your space. Basically, you get to take all your treasures and decorations and hang them together on a single wall. An eye for detail and spacing is useful in a project like this in order to keep your wall from being too overwhelming. Don't worry, though, because it's easy to test what your wall will look like before you commit to hanging anything up! First, you'll want to take out everything you want to include in your gallery wall and measure each item. Then, using printer paper, wrapping paper, newspaper, or whatever you have handy, cut pieces of paper in the same sizes as your decorations. Tape the paper on your wall and spend time arranging and rearranging your papers until you find the configuration that you like best. Then, simply hang up your decorations in their assigned spots. Gallery walls bring together the best parts of clutter and order to create beautiful decor.

THE TRAY'S THE THING: If you have space on your coffee table or dining table, get a tray (or a large plate) and arrange part of your collection there. Not only will it look fancy to have your trinkets on their own special tray, but it's easy to move them somewhere else if you're hosting a dinner party for your goblin friends and you need the table space. Putting your collection of colored glass bottles, or ceramic animals, or moss terrariums on a tray will add depth to your space, since it moves your collections away from the walls and shelves toward the center of your room. You can even display your jars on your tray! That's two displays in one! If you have a tray, you can truly have it all.

When you're putting together your various displays, consider grouping similar items near one another. Rather than scattering your plastic dinosaurs around your house, put them all on your TV console. Instead of hanging a few keys from your antique key collection on your fridge, hang them all up next to each other on the wall above your desk. It's fun to try different ways of displaying your collections.

GOBLIN MINIMALISM

If you're an organized person who's beginning to doubt
whether you're allowed to be a goblin, worry not. You can be
a goblin and decorate in the goblin style even if you deep-clean
your house once a month and you love using a label maker.
Clutter doesn't have to mean "all-out mess." Even organized
weirdos can decorate in the goblin style, and it's no harder
than embracing other decor. Here are some tips for creating
controlled chaos.

🍄 **Control your clutter:** If you don't like the idea of your space being
overwhelmed with trinkets, tchotchkes, and treasures, focus on just
a few smaller areas to display your cache. Designate one wall as a
gallery wall and leave your other walls blank. Add just one or two
decorations to your bookshelf. Keep all your full jars and bottles on
the windowsill instead of scattered around. It's okay to have some
guardrails around your clutter—you can still show off all your favorite things without feeling like they're overwhelming your space.

Simple yet strange: Who says that minimalism can only be beige and boring? If you're a diehard fan of the clean and uncomplicated, you can still integrate the weirdness of goblin sensibilities into your decor. If you're committed to having only one thing on each wall, why not swing for a butterfly specimen box instead of a poster, or a cloth you dyed yourself with blueberry juice instead of a store-bought tapestry? Instead of a single cream-colored chair in the corner, you could go for a single green velvet chair in the corner. Find a weird lamp instead of a mid-century modern one or make a seashell mobile to serve as a focal point. Indulge your weird, playful, unexpected tastes no matter what type of decor suits you best. There's no one way to do minimalism right, just like there's no one way to be a goblin.

You do you: Remember that, ultimately, goblin decor is about making your space feel cozy and safe for you. If the thing that makes you most comfortable is having a clean and clutter-free space, embrace that! Redesignating your clutter as decor might make you feel better about displaying your favorite items, but even if you like to keep your things tucked away, it doesn't mean you can't be a goblin. It's totally goblin-friendly to keep your things cleaned up so you can bring them out whenever you need or want them. There are all kinds of goblins in the world, and the goblin community is grateful for all of them.

The Life-Changing Magic of Not Tidying Up

What does it mean to live in a clean home? Does it mean you disinfect every surface every day? That you only have the bare minimum supplies needed to live? That you drag a vacuum behind you everywhere you go? Or can it mean that your space is organized in a way that makes sense to you, that you know where (most) of your belongings are, that your dishes are usually put away and there isn't stray grime growing in any corners?

In general, we all need to give ourselves a break. There's a lot of moral weight put on keeping your space clean, but *clean* isn't an objective term. For some people, a clean space is one where everything is put away and scrubbed once a week. For others, a clean space might just mean that you can see a majority of the floor. There's nothing inherently good about being clean, or bad about being messy. Clean and messy aren't moral binaries, they're just ways of living with your stuff. The amount of sweaters and costume jewelry you have on your bed at any one time doesn't determine what kind of person you are or how deserving you are of love, care, and attention.

Even people who love cleaning sometimes have a week or month or even a year where they just don't want to clean regularly. That's okay! That doesn't mean you'll never do laundry again, or that you've somehow become morally reprehensible. Nothing in life is concrete, and accepting the fluidity of your energy and motivation levels will make you feel much better. You don't need to live your life according to other people's standards. Just keep your space in a state that feels safe, comfortable, and accessible to you, and don't worry about whether or not a stranger would deem it "clean enough."

Instead of morally weighted ideas about cleanliness, goblins can embrace a more person-centered approach. Does your space feel livable? Does it suit your needs? Does the level of clutter feel homey and familiar to you, or does it stress you out? Is there actual *dirt*, in a way that might threaten your health or the health of your guests, or is there simply *mess*? Your version of cleanliness doesn't need to look like everyone else's. Finding your own definition of clean is an opportunity to explore what makes you feel safe and relaxed in your home.

If you're feeling frustrated with your lack of organization, or if your clutter is getting in the way, it's great to seek out guidance and tips for cleaning that work for you—whether that means enlisting friends who love organization to help you rethink your closet and pantry, or paying someone to occasionally clean your apartment for you. Keeping your space tidy, or at least organized according to your particular needs, can be a reflection of your care for yourself and your living environment. Our space can have an impact on our mental health, and it's worth it to consider whether you're someone who loves having clothes laying everywhere, or someone who feels anxious and depressed if they have a messy closet. So, what are some ways to create a habitat that best suits your needs?

Know where it goes. Instead of putting important items in "safe places" and then immediately forgetting where they are, try designating certain places as forever homes for your important items. For example, rather than leaving your phone charger wherever you last charged your phone, try keeping it only one place all the time, specifically a place that you use and see often. Put a hook on the wall and always hang your keys there. Leave a jar next to every chair, couch, or bed in your apartment and always put your reading glasses in one of those jars when you're done using them. Don't make this hard for yourself; choose simple, obvious places, and even consider keeping a note on your phone of where everything goes as you're learning where you like to have these forever homes. If you're having a hard time deciding where to put things, use the concept of "put a bin under it": when you notice yourself consistently gathering piles of stuff in a particular spot, put a bin (or your preferred type of storage) in that spot and boom! No more pile, just a nice bin.

Clutter has its place. Every single nook and cranny of your space doesn't need to be labeled and vacuum-sealed in order for you to be organized. The trick to organization is having designated places for your mess. When you get the mail, you don't need to stack it in alphabetical order and put it in a binder. You can keep a plate or a flower pot or a placemat on the table to serve as a spot to drop your mail. That way, your letters can stay messy,  but the mess is contained to one designated spot (put a bin under it!). Plus, it makes it easier to find what you're looking for later on. You can do this with anything: keep things you always take with you in a bowl by your front door, fill a mug with spare lip balms and lotions, leave a jar in the bathroom for loose jewelry. Being organized is about making your important items memorable and accessible. This method can also help you keep track of when you need to refill or cut back on certain items. If your mail pile is looking more like a mail skyscraper, it might be time to go through that stack. If your mug of pens is empty, you may need to invest in new pens. If you stick with your organizational habits, they can remove some of the pressure of having to remember everything.

Have fun with it. The idea of making cleaning fun might sound trite or even impossible. However, if you struggle with tidying and organization and want to improve, it's worth thinking of ways to make these tasks less painful. Think about what motivates you in other areas of your life, and try to apply those motivation tactics to cleaning. If you work best in ten-minute increments, then break up your cleaning process accordingly. If you can only do one task at a time before getting bored, plan on doing laundry one day and scrubbing the bathroom another. Putting on a show, a podcast, or music or even calling a friend while you work can also help make the process more enjoyable. If you want to clean more, clean in a way that works for you. Don't worry about scrubbing down your entire apartment in an hour, or strictly scheduling a cleaning day once a week. Instead, work in the way that feels the most pleasant to you. Make the work work for you, instead of the other way around.

MOSS WALL ART

Looking for the perfect goblin centerpiece for your eclectic new gallery wall? Look no further than moss wall art. This decor craft is a great way to bring no-maintenance greenery into your space and show off your fun, naturalist, goblin sensibilities. Moss wall art is cheap to make but beautiful to look at—and that's the goblin ideal!

WHAT YOU'LL NEED

- ★ A sheet of paper and a pencil
- ★ A frame, or a flat piece of wood
- ★ Preserved moss (This will be available at most craft and plant stores. Make sure to buy preserved moss and not live moss, because live moss will need lots of upkeep and moisture that could damage your walls.)
- ★ Scissors
- ★ Hot-glue gun, or wood glue
- ★ Foam board (optional)
- ★ Sticks, stones, and preserved flowers (optional)

WHAT TO DO

1. Sketch the design you'd like to achieve on a piece of paper. You don't need to perfectly recreate your design, but it's nice to have some idea of what you want before you get started. If you want to create a lot of depth in your moss art, cut out pieces of foam board and glue them to your frame. This way, some of your moss will be elevated. You don't need to do this, but it's a nice touch!

2. If you're using a picture frame, carefully remove the glass from the frame so you're left with just the back and edges.

3. Take your moss and cut or tear it into the shapes you want. Start laying and arranging your moss until you're happy with your design.

4. Glue down your moss. If you're using wood glue, spread a thin layer over the back of the frame or foam board. Wood glue bonds well with the moss, but note that it can take a full day to dry! If you're using a hot-glue gun, simply apply your glue to the back of each moss piece before you lay it on the frame.

5. If you want to add more to your moss art, take your sticks, rocks, preserved flowers, or whatever other goblin decorations you gathered and glue them down as well.

6. Let your glue dry, and you're done!

Going Beyond the Visual

What makes a home cozy? Is it strictly Instagram-worthiness—whatever qualities of ambience make it show up well in a photo on a social feed? Or does coziness go deeper than just visual appeal? Of course, it's nice to have a space that looks good—but everyone knows that. What a lot of people forget to consider when decorating their lair is the importance of textures, smells, and sounds in their home. Your space should ideally appeal to several of your senses, not just one. Let's think about what we can add to your environment that makes it cozy but isn't immediately visible in a photo.

TEXTURES

Adding pleasant textures to your space is a great way to immediately amp up the coziness. Especially if you have a lot of specific sensory preferences and aversions, spending time thinking about the textures of your space can make your life significantly more enjoyable in the long run. Try walking around your apartment and touching all your blankets, sheets, rugs, and towels. Do you love the feeling of any of them? Do you hate the feeling of others? Take some notes about which fabrics you prefer and which you find unpalatable.

If there are certain items that you can't stand the texture of, then get rid of them! Maybe you can host a goblin blanket swap or just donate them to a thrift store. There's no reason to keep something that's making you actively uncomfortable. If there are items that have really great textures, try keeping them more readily available. If you have a throw blanket that you love but it's always buried under your bed, try keeping it on your bed or sofa instead. Always keep your comfort accessible.

Although we spend a lot of time thinking about what textures our hands like, it's also worth thinking about which textures other parts of our bodies like. For example, if you hate getting out of bed and stepping onto the cold floor, maybe find a rug or bath mat or even a pair of slippers to keep next to your bed. If your back gets sore sitting in your work chair, try adding some pillows that offer back support. If you wash your face with a washcloth that feels too rough, swap it out for something softer. Prioritizing your comfort means taking a minute or two to make yourself feel better in any given situation and especially in your own home.

SMELLS

Whether you love or hate fragrances, most people have a strong opinion about having smells in their space. For some people, burning a candle is soothing, while for others it can trigger an allergy attack. Because of this, you'll want to check with any roommates you might have before you start using more (or fewer) smells in your room. (Yes, you can aim for fewer smells! If you want a scent-free environment, that's just as valid as having a handful of carefully placed candles. What's important is establishing the sensory landscape that makes you feel the most comfortable.)

If you're someone who loves smells, scented candles are an obvious choice—but candles can be a fire hazard and they're not allowed in every building. If you're someone who can't have candles for whatever reason, there are plenty of other ways to introduce scent into your environment. A quick visit to the grocery store should offer you dozens of options for scented aerosol spray, scented plug-ins, and the like. These are a great, quick way to bring a lot of scent into your space. But if they're too strong, try scent sticks or diffusers, or even go ahead and make your own potpourri. There are tons of nonflammable ways to make your space smell good (check out page 192 for more ideas).

Regardless of what kind of scent enhancer you choose, your next step will be deciding on your favorite smells. Check out any scented items you already own—air fresheners and candles, but also perfumes, deodorants, and soaps. You probably already gravitate toward a certain genre of fragrance, whether or not you've noticed before. Think about what all your favorite smells have in common: Are they all floral or do you lean musky? Do you like sweet smells or do you prefer spicy? Investigate which types of scents you prefer so you can narrow down your scent choices later on.

If you want to get a little bougie, keep in mind that most fancy (or homemade) candle companies have smells that go way beyond your typical flowers and baked goods fare. You can find candles that are scented like dirt, old books, petrichor, garlic, wood smoke—if your favorite smell isn't a traditionally "good" smell, there's a good chance you'll be able to find a candle of it if you do a quick internet search for "[your desired smell] + candle." Even if you can't find your favorite smell online, some cities have candle labs where you can mix your own scents!

Once you've discovered your ideal genre of scent, do a little research to find out which ingredients are often used in the type of scent you prefer. For example, tobacco and amber are common ingredients in spicy scents, while patchouli is the primary ingredient in most musky scents. Knowing which ingredients go into your favorite scents is going to make shopping for candles and other scented items a lot easier (especially if you're shopping online).

Now that you have a sense of which scents you like, consider: why make your apartment smell the same everywhere? Why not pick different scents for different spaces? Get gardenia air freshener for the bathroom, a tobacco candle for next to the TV, and lavender potpourri to keep next to your bed. Experiment with how different scents go together, and layer scents for more depth. Change your go-to scents with each season or for holidays to get you in the spirit. Another fun thing about trying out different smells is learning how they make you feel. If the scent of honeycomb makes you feel calm while you work, keep a honeycomb candle near your desk. Light a citrusy candle when you wake up if that smell boosts your mood. As with everything, make your scents work for you. And if you get tired of the way your space smells, switch it up!

SOUNDS

Sound isn't something that immediately comes to mind when we think of decorating but it can have a huge effect on the feeling of a space. What kinds of sounds do you want in your ideal goblin lair? What kinds of sounds do you *not* want? If you can't stand repetitive sounds, but you have a clock on your desk, it's probably hard to focus. If your alarm is set to an irritating sound, you might be waking up in a bad mood every day. Little sounds like these can impact our moods and routines so much that it's worth thinking about the soundscape of your space before you completely finish your nest.

First, think large-scale with your sounds. Do you like having some ambient sounds in the background of your life? Do you prefer having music or a podcast playing all the time? If so, it might be worth investing in a speaker, noise machine, or fan to create that background noise you're looking for. If you don't want to buy a speaker, you can always put your phone in a cup or mug to amplify the sound. Regardless of how you amplify them, think about which sounds make you feel calm, which ones help you focus, and which ones help you wake up. If you prefer silence, that's great! But if not, try experimenting with different background sounds at different parts of your day to find out which ones feel best to you. Remember, there's probably not one single sound that'll make you feel good all day, so don't be afraid to mix things up.

Next, think about the smaller sounds in your life: a creaky door, a loud watch, an annoying ringtone. What can you do to improve those little noises that you hear every day, multiple times a day? They'll probably only take two minutes to fix, and taking the time to improve something that's been bothering you is going to make you feel so much better. It can be hard to feel motivated to do small tasks like this, but especially if you're a person who's sensitive to sounds, it's going to be worth it. Why suffer with a screeching timer sound when you could have your favorite movie theme play every time you've finished a task?

Goblins Without Green Thumbs: A Support Group

Since goblins generally love nature and plants, anyone who lacks plant proficiency might feel a bit left out of the culture. Having greenery around is great, and it fits the goblin vibe perfectly, but there's more than one way to introduce plants to your space. If you have don't have a green thumb so much as a pile of dead plants in your backyard, it could be useful to think of alternate ways of living out your natural, crunchy goblin dreams. Luckily, there's no shortage of alternatives for greening up your space even if you can't green up your thumb.

LOW-MAINTENANCE PLANTS

If you're really sold on the idea of keeping living plants in your space, try getting some low-maintenance plants before you commit to anything that needs more regular care. Succulents (like cactuses, jade plants, and aloe vera), air plants, and some common houseplants like snake plants, spider plants, and ZZ plants are simple to care for and hard to kill. If you buy a plant that needs soil to live, do a little bit of research about which soil to fill that plant's pot with. (Most desert plants prefer a sandier soil, for instance.) Keeping your plant in the little plastic cup and dead soil you bought it in isn't going to do the plant any favors.

Repotting in fresh soil with lots of nutrients is a simple trick to help your plants survive longer. If you buy an air plant, you don't need to worry about soil, which is great! Just remember to keep up with the watering. If your plant looks and feels dry, that means it's due for a drink. If it looks totally fine but you're bored and want to water a plant, find something else to do! Don't kill your plant by overwatering due to anxiety or boredom. Even though these plants are low-maintenance, it doesn't mean they can't die. But don't worry: as you get to know your plant better, you'll get a better sense of what it wants and when. Plants are decent at communicating their needs.

FAKE PLANTS

This is a great option for the goblins who know that, no matter how low-maintenance a plant is, they'll still kill it. Fake plants are impossible to kill, they never wilt, and you don't have to deal with watering or dirt or fungus gnats (the little fruit-fly-type pests that can spawn from real plants). Fake plants can be found at most craft stores and home goods stores. Although you might have visions of ugly plastic flower displays, fake plants are actually a very cute and flexible piece of decor that'll add green to your space without the hassle. They come in all kinds of plant types, so if you're not a flower person, you can always pick up some fake succulents or even a large fake monstera.

Try using fake plants less as attention-grabbing focal pieces and more as detail work. For a pop of greenery here and there, try placing small items like an old glass bottle with two or three fake flowers or a row of fake cactuses on a high shelf. People are less likely to notice that your plants are fake if the satin petals aren't sitting inches away. You can also break out your creative side and try your hand at flower (or leaf/stem/twig) arranging. Creating visually interesting arrangements with your fake plants will also take some of the focus off their fakeness and put it onto your impressive ability to put together a beautiful bouquet. The biggest thing that will make your fake plants look real, though, is mixing them in with a few real plants. If you keep a mix of easy-to-care-for plants and fake plants, nobody will ever notice which ones are real and which ones aren't.

MAKE YOUR OWN PLANTS

If you're the kind of goblin who can't keep a plant alive but still wants to get their hands dirty, you can try making your own plants. Using paper, felt, cardboard, or even papier-mâché, you can create beautiful and unique plants that you'll never need to worry about killing. You don't need to worry about these plants looking hyperrealistic because part of the fun of making your own plants is having pieces of greenery that look like cool, homemade art. Embrace the artsy, homemade aesthetic and lean into the playfulness that handmade plants will add to your space. (For more, see page 114.)

If you're not a fan of art projects, you can display dried plants in your space. Strings of dried roses hanging from a wall or vases of dry dahlias will add a nice natural touch to your home with little effort. It's easy to dry flowers by simply hanging them upside down for a week or so, and you could even press leaves and flowers in a book to use for other decor later. Dry flowers add a bit of witchiness to any space, so they're perfect for goblins.

PAPER FERNS

So, you're interested in adding some greenery to your space without getting dirt under your nails. Well, you're in luck, because it's fun and easy to make plants out of paper! Paper ferns are great because they don't take long to make but they'll offer that green you're looking for, along with some wonderful natural shapes. Plus, they cost almost nothing! Once you get the hang of making these paper ferns, you'll be able to decorate your whole home with the perfect paper greenery.

WHAT YOU'LL NEED

- ★ Green crepe paper streamer
- ★ Thick wire (aim for around 2 mm or 14 gauge)
- ★ Wire cutters
- ★ Scissors
- ★ Glue stick
- ★ Hot-glue gun

If you want to make your ferns look as though they're growing, get a plant pot or a vase and put a foam ball inside. Then, cover the ball with preserved moss and stick the wire at the end of your ferns through the moss into the ball. Now you have a cute, natural-looking display for your ferns!

WHAT TO DO

1. Cut a piece of crepe paper between 8 and 10 inches long and fold in half lengthwise.

2. With wire cutters, cut a piece of wire to be about 2 inches longer than your paper.

3. With scissors, cut an arc from the bottom of the paper to the top (make sure you're not cutting the folded side!), so that the paper will come to a point when unfolded. (This is like cutting the bottom part of a Valentine's heart.)

4. With the paper still folded, make a series of cuts from the outside toward the folded side. The cuts should be about ¼ inch apart, but they can be spaced wider if you want wider leaves. Make sure you stop at least ⅛ inch from the folded edge.

5. Round the edges of each of your cuts to make your fern leaves look more natural.

6. Cut another piece of crepe paper the length of your wire, cut in half lengthwise, and cover with glue stick. Roll it around the wire so the wire is completely covered.

7. Unfold the first piece of paper and apply hot glue down the fold at the center of your fern. Place your wire in the glue.

8. Fluff the leaves and bend the fern until it looks good!

Do you feel ready to make your own home into a goblin lair now? If you're feeling overwhelmed, start with small things, like noting what you already like about your room or hanging up a few of the watercolors you've been doing of local flora. You don't need to change everything about your home in a day. Take your time and be intentional about how you create your new habitat. Consider all different aspects of hominess covered in this chapter, from organization to collection presentation to incorporation of pleasing scents and textures. There's a lot to think about when you're making a home, but that's the way it should be. A lair is a sacred space, after all. It's a representation of you, and you weren't built in a day either.

If you're filled with ideas for your lair, that's great! Spend some time with your ideas, really flesh them out, and think about how it would feel to live in your newly redesigned space. Sometimes you can come up with an idea right away that seems really neat, like stacking a bunch of ant farms on top of each other to create a glorious wall of ant farms. But then on second thought, you end up wondering where you'd get all those ants, and how well you'd realistically be able to take care of them, and what you'd do if something happened and all your ants escaped and took over your apartment. Some ideas are better as jumping-off points for other ideas. You want your habitat to be perfect for the real you, not an idea of you who's really into ants.

However you choose to decorate your home, make sure to be deliberate about your choices. You want this to be a place where you feel good and safe and welcomed. Having a goblin lair is less about introducing a lot of earth tones and mushrooms to your space and more about creating a space that feels like a unique extension of yourself. No matter how small or large your home is, there's always room for it to become your perfect goblin lair if you're intentional and true to yourself. If you give yourself the gift of a thoughtful, treasured home, you'll receive infinite comfort in return.

CHAPTER 5

Frogs and Toads Are Friends

What you can learn
from the weird little animals
in your life

L isten, we all love dogs and cats. We all love bunnies and hamsters and all the other furry, sweet little friends who deign to give us their company. No one is trying to argue against dogs and cats and the like. But! Have you ever considered that there are scaly, slimy, or exoskeletoned creatures who might also make good friends, companions, and role models? Why does fur get all the love?

If you're the kind of person who's always felt like a lizard in a world of mammals, you're not alone. Not everyone can be, or even wants to be, a golden retriever type of person (read: someone excitable, loyal, sweet) or a cat type of person (read: someone independent, mysterious, rebellious). Some of us are frogs (chill, flexible) or turtles (thoughtful, kind) or even hermit crabs (anxious little guys).

Being a goblin is all about learning to embrace the weird and unexpected, both in nature and in yourself. Furry animals are easy to love, but taking the time to learn about and appreciate the slimier animals is central to the goblin way of life. Embracing these creatures can also help you embrace the things about yourself that you aren't totally in love with. What can we learn about ourselves from lizards or snakes or poison frogs? How can learning to love animals that are outside of the mainstream help us love our own oddities?

Just like witches have familiars, goblins have slimy, scaly friends to help them navigate the world and point them in the direction of the most wonderfully weird parts of life. Fur gets all the love, but sliminess can teach us about confidence, care for others, self-acceptance, gender, and what it looks like to create space for yourself in a big, mushy, humid world.

Find Your Creature Role Model

Horoscopes and zodiac signs are great if you like that sort of thing, but there's no better guide for a goblin's life than a weird little animal. The stars are far away but snails and snakes and hermit crabs are right at your feet, and they can teach you a lot about yourself. Are you a lizard sun with a turtle rising, or do you relate more to your axolotl moon? Read through to find out which slimy, scaly, or shelled creature you can most relate to, and use that as a jumping-off point to consider how you view yourself and what you enjoy.

FROG

If you're a frog, you're pretty hard to upset. Real frogs are chill and unbothered by the things that are happening around them. They like to stay in their lane and focus on themselves. If you're a frog, you're probably the type of friend who needs the friend group drama explained to them several times before they actually remember it, but you're always available if anyone involved needs somebody to talk to. Frogs are really just vibing, and they're as happy being part of a group as they are alone.

- **Likes**: Vibing, driving around at night, cozy video games, crunchy snacks, hearing about drama

- **Dislikes**: Getting dragged into drama, loud noises, being hungry

- **Hobbies**: Maintaining an impressive moisturizer collection, curating hyperspecific playlists, cooking simple but amazing food

TURTLE

Turtles are thoughtful and caring and always down to hang. Although it might seem like turtles are shy since they're often retreating into their shells, they're actually just taking a minute to think over what's going on around them. The big circle shapes on turtle shells are called scutes, which is short for "so cute" (the second part may not technically be true). If you're a turtle, you may need some time to work out the best course of action or the right thing to say next, and that's okay! Because taking a second to figure out what to do next is what allows turtles to be such kind friends.

- **Likes:** Noise-canceling headphones, affection, fresh fruit, ASMR, fancy lip balm, small but thoughtful gifts from friends

- **Dislikes:** Being ignored, grocery shopping, making quick decisions

- **Hobbies:** Rewatching their favorite TV shows, any and all crafts, does intensely dedicating yourself to a new hobby every two weeks count as one hobby?

SNAIL

Snails are the archetypal homebodies, but don't let that fool you into thinking they aren't also curious. These little guys are the definition of moisturized, and it's because they really know how to take care of themselves. They actually produce their own skin products (yes, people use snail slime for skincare)! Snails are perfectly comfortable staying at home, because they've made their home a cozy space that makes them feel safe. However, they love learning about the world and as long as they feel secure, they can be great explorers.

Although snails love their homes, they know the truth of the world: that home is wherever they are.

- **Likes**: Soft pillows, novelty earrings, well-organized bookshelves, crystals, round mugs

- **Dislikes**: Gender, fluorescent lights, being bored

- **Hobbies**: Skincare, looking at expensive houses online, hosting dinner parties

LIZARD

Lizards are surprisingly outgoing for cold-blooded creatures. They're equally happy hanging out in the sun or sitting at home, as long as they have some friends around. If you're a lizard, you love to be involved, for better or worse, and often find yourself at the center of a room rather than the corner. You prefer feeling like the main character whenever possible, but you know that no reptile is an island and you love supporting your friends as well.

- **Likes:** Getting texts, disco balls, parties, statement pieces, gossip

- **Dislikes:** Being alone, boring coffee orders, traffic

- **Hobbies:** Inviting friends over, filming makeup tutorials they'll never show anyone, collecting things

AXOLOTL

Hello, beautiful weirdos. Axolotls are some of the strangest little friends you can have. Your axolotl friends will always encourage you to take the road less traveled or try the hobby you never considered before. (But guess what? It turns out you're weirdly good at that hobby. Thanks, axolotl!) These salamanders go through life on their own terms and aren't often swayed by peer pressure or public opinion. That said, they're often more insecure than they let on—sometimes they do things their own way not to be a rebel but because it's all they know. Axolotls benefit from friends who will affirm their unexpected fashion choices and support their unconventional lifestyles, but who will also offer some grounding when needed.

- **Likes:** Bold prints, handmade everything, neon lights, pop-up books, fun facts

- **Dislikes:** Capitalism, long movies, following recipes

- **Hobbies:** Sitting in chairs weirdly, collecting indie press books, finding new hobbies

HERMIT CRAB

Hermit crabs are the definition of little guys. They're cute and strange and they love scuttling around in a way that's both charming and a little weird. Hermit crab types are as loveable as they are anxious, as delightful as they are tense. They have a tendency to overthink everything, and this often leads them to distress. Hermit crabs need friends who can remind them that not everything is that deep and offer a shoulder to cry on if necessary. Luckily, hermit crabs are so sweet that it's easy for them to make good friends.

- **Likes:** Comfy couches, tea parties, tissue boxes, reusable water bottles, sweet treats

- **Dislikes:** Waking up early, feeling rushed, taking out the trash

- **Hobbies:** Writing letters to friends, reading romance novels, keeping their fridge fully stocked

SNAKE

Snakes are always on the go. They're hardworking and focused, and they feel best when their nose is to the grindstone. It can be hard to convince a snake type to chill out, but once they do, they'll work as hard on chilling out as they did on whatever project they were just focused on. Snakes love having a few close friends who can remind them when to take a break, and in return a snake's friends are rewarded with intense care and loyalty that makes everyone's lives better.

- **Likes:** A full calendar, fancy pens, anxiety medication, finding a simple way to do a complex task

- **Dislikes:** A messy workspace, when friends don't answer texts, finishing a book they don't like

- **Hobbies:** Running tabletop RPGs, hoarding loose-leaf teas, keeping their email inbox empty

Introducing: Some Cool Frogs

If you opened this book hoping to find some dope amphibians, your wish is about to come true. Some people might see a frog and be freaked out by their bulbous eyes, their slimy skin, their bizarre tongue, or many other weird and disconcerting physical traits that frogs possess. But goblins know the truth about frogs: They're so cool. They're actually so incredibly cool. From their impressive range of colors and appearances to their jumping prowess to their strange croaking call, frogs are particularly interesting animals who deserve all the love we can give them.

Because all frogs are so neat, it's hard to choose just a handful to represent here as the coolest of all. Hopefully you'll find your favorite frog species represented, but if you don't, just consider it an honorable mention. In fact, all frogs are honorable mentions to this list of coolest frogs for the simple fact that all frogs are cool. Now that that's been made official, it's frog time.

- **Hairy frog:** There's a reason this frog is also known as the "horror frog"—it's just so spooky looking. Looking at this frog is like the opposite of ASMR. Some things are simply not meant to have hair! Although it's not really hair—the hair like structures that grow on male hairy frogs are actually a kind of gills, so the male frog can stay underwater for longer to watch over his eggs. So don't worry; if you thought the hair was gross, you'll be glad to know that it's actually a collection of tissue and arteries that act like external gills. On second thought, that's a lot worse.

- **Poison frogs:** Every kid who ever had an interest in amphibians knows about these guys, the hotties of the frog world. They're small, cute, beautifully colored, and wildly toxic. There's just something so satisfying about a creature that's equally as cute as it is poisonous. These frogs secrete poison from their skin, so just touching one can have adverse effects. In fact, the golden poison frog is considered one of the most toxic animals on earth. Poison frogs prove what all goblins know: big power can come in small packages.

- **Flying frogs:** If you thought regular jumping frogs were cool, get ready for . . . frogs that can fly. Okay, so technically they do more gliding than flying, but still. The most well-known flying frog species has webbed fingers and extra skin between its limbs so that it can glide between trees and parachute to the ground. These frogs can glide up to fifty feet, which is especially impressive when you consider that they're only about three inches long. These frogs are dreamers: they weren't satisfied with simply walking or jumping, so they took matters into their own sticky little fingers. Impressive.

- **Leaf frogs:** The Malayan leaf frog looks, as you may have guessed, like a leaf. These frogs like to hide in the leaves that cover the rainforest floor—a perfect hiding place for an animal that evolved to look like a little leaf on the rainforest floor. They have two points on their heads that look like horns, which proves that these frogs are incredibly fashionable. In the frog family, what could be a better look than leaf chic plus horns? Leaf frogs know how to dress for their environment.

- **Cute little baby squeaky frogs:** Okay, so this frog is technically called the desert rain frog, but they *are* cute, little, and squeaky, so this name isn't *wrong*. These sweet little guys emit a frightening battle cry that sounds similar to a squeaky toy. Desert rain frogs are round and perfect, but they're also slightly weird even for frogs. They live in burrows in the desert, and they don't need to live in water to survive. They're also too round to hop, so they just walk around instead. Goblins are sure to relate to a frog that's adorable, perfect, and also quite strange.

FROG COIN PURSE

If you're looking for a way to keep your goblin familiar with you at all times, try making a frog coin purse. This craft is great because not only does it let you show off your love of your favorite amphibian, it's also the perfect place to store little treasures—rocks, leaves, movie tickets, notes, and, yes, even coins—that you find throughout your day. It's always a good idea to keep a mini goblin hoard on you, just in case. The best thing about this craft is that it's extremely simple and cheap to make. It should take less than a half hour to put together, and then you're free to spend the rest of your day filling it with treasures.

WHAT YOU'LL NEED

- ★ A square or square-ish envelope
- ★ Felt or scrap fabric (preferably green or otherwise frog colored)
- ★ Marker
- ★ Scissors
- ★ Hot-glue gun
- ★ Velcro fastener dots
- ★ Googly eyes

WHAT TO DO

1. Unfold your envelope completely so it's a flat piece of paper.

2. Place your unfolded envelope on top of your fabric, trace the shape of the unfolded envelope onto the fabric with your marker, and cut it out. You should have a shape that's roughly a diamond, with one corner cut off.

3. Turn your fabric so the underside of the fabric is facing up and the flat corner is pointing toward you. Fold the left and right corners into each other and glue their points together just where the points meet. Make sure you don't glue the points to the back of your fabric.

4. Line the bottom corner with glue and flip it up to adhere to the folded-in corners. (You're rebuilding the shape of the original envelope.)

5. Glue a Velcro dot to the underside of your top corner, and another Velcro dot to the flat corner, in a place where all the corners meet.

6. Time to decorate! Glue the googly eyes to the top of your coin purse, so it looks like a frog face. Feel free to get creative with it! Add a felt tongue, or glue on some sparkles.

7. You're done! Have fun feeding your frog friend all the treasures you find on your adventures.

Slimy Celebrities

Mainstream society isn't ready to acknowledge this, but as a culture we seem to have a keen interest in reptiles and amphibians. From Kermit to the Teenage Mutant Ninja Turtles, these little guys pop up everywhere in our media. We're obsessed with these slimy, scaly weirdos. These creatures might be a little odd, a little sticky, and sometimes even a little toxic, but deep down they're neat animals who are extremely important to our ecosystems. It's good that they get a lot of free, positive publicity. Goblins can learn a lot from these animals, so let's hop into discussing some fictional reptiles and amphibians and the lessons they've taught us.

- **Frog and Toad**: Both of these loveable storybook characters have plenty of lessons for goblins. These lessons include: why it's important to eat a lot of cookies, how to write a letter to a friend, and the beauty of admiring a nice day. However, the best lesson Frog and Toad teach is, of course, how to love the people (or amphibians) closest to you. Frog and Toad are always thinking of each other, considering each other's needs in addition to their own, and showing they care for each other every time they're together.

- **The Mixed-Up Chameleon**: The hero of Eric Carle's classic children's book is a bored chameleon who wants to try something new after seeing all the great animals at the zoo. Bored and looking for something new is definitely a relatable feeling, but most of us don't have the ability to literally morph parts of our bodies into radically new shapes. We can, however, start wearing a bunch of dark eyeliner in an attempt to be goth, or get really into sauteing vegetables in an attempt to be a vegetarian, or only wear clothing styles that were popular in the 1960s in an attempt to seem like a time traveler and confuse old people. The Mixed-Up Chameleon would encourage you to try it all, because sometimes you need to try things to find out what doesn't work. Sure, the ultimate moral of the book is that it's better to be yourself, but how does the chameleon learn about himself? By trying lots of new things. Go ahead, dye your hair, start riding a bike everywhere, and only wear cowboy boots. How're you going to know what works for you if you never try?

- **Kermit the Frog**: Probably the most well-known amphibian in all of pop culture, Kermit is the long-limbed, big-eyed, green everyman of the Muppets. He loves playing banjo and sorting out disagreements, and his greatest accomplishment is getting Miss Piggy to fall in love with him. Kermit is an easy character to learn from, because he's likable and funny and level headed and a very talented songwriter. One of Kermit's best lessons is that leadership doesn't always look intrusive and overwhelming. As he displays, good leadership is about listening to people, apologizing when you need to, and trying to do what's best by your friends and co-workers while taking their feelings into account.

- **The Teenage Mutant Ninja Turtles**: Leonardo, Raphael, Donatello, and Michelangelo were just four normal baby turtles until exposure to toxic waste turned them into crime-fighting superheroes (and also teenagers). The TMNT live in the sewers below New York City and are known for their skills in ninjutsu, their love of pizza, and their totally radical way with words. Even though the turtles are constantly tasked with saving New York, they always stay upbeat and happy. No matter how many times Shredder concocts a bogus plan to take over the world, the TMNT are not only ready to stop him but willing to have fun while they do it. In situations that would drive most people to break out in stress-induced hives, the brothers usually end up having a pretty good time and getting pizza afterward. We can all learn some chill from the Teenage Mutant Ninja Turtles. Sometimes situations look scary, but once you're actually in them, they end up being no big deal. Maybe we should all try our best to take things a little less seriously, and we might feel a little more bodacious.

- Flick: This punk, bug-obsessed red chameleon in *Animal Crossing: New Horizons* is always a welcome visitor to our fictional islands. He loves to wax poetic about all kinds of bugs and has been known to get lost in thought when considering the beauty and grandeur of an Atlas moth. He's also a talented artist who loves making replicas of the insects and arachnids you sell him. (He's also definitely in a relationship with CJ, his roommate/partner/fishing-enthusiast beaver, right? Right.) Anyone who's played *Animal Crossing* knows about Flick's impressive reverence for the natural world, something that's both endearing and enviable. What if we could all walk around like Flick, driven to distraction by the beauty of the world around us? What if we all took the time to notice how lovely even the smallest, most ignored parts of nature are? Flick reminds us to keep our sense of wonder intact (especially when it comes to bugs).

- Loveland Frog: Does a cryptid count as being part of pop culture? For the sake of this list, let's say yes. The Loveland Frog is a four-foot-tall frog who lives in Ohio and walks around on its hind legs like a person. Pretty cool, right? Just a child-sized frog wandering around the Ohio river system, scaring teens and startling the cops. There are endless lessons that goblins can learn from this amphibious cryptid, such as how to strike terror into the heart of a community, how to piss off the police, and how to become an icon in Ohio. But perhaps the best lesson that can be taught by the Loveland Frog is that no matter how weird you may be, there's always people out there who are looking for someone just like you. Just like the people of Cincinnati love the Loveland Frog, there are people out there who will love you for exactly who you are.

BUG BUDDIES

So you want a weird pet, but you're not interested in the usual lineup of frogs, lizards, and snakes. Have you considered . . . bugs? Bugs are great because they don't take up a ton of space and they're generally cheaper to care for than reptiles and amphibians. Some bugs are high-maintenance, but let's assume you're starting out with some simple bugs who don't need much of anything except your love and care. Insects, arachnids, and all kinds of creepy-crawlies can make great pets for goblins who prefer their familiars to have exoskeletons. Here are some great bugs for beginners.

🍄 **Praying mantises:** There are few insects cooler than a praying mantis. With their green coloring, their big eyes, their strange bent arms, and their hidden wings, mantises make beautiful pets. As a bonus, they only require a small tank with a screen top, a layer of soil, and some plants and branches for a habitat. However, they are cannibals, so you don't want to keep more than one in a single tank. If you keep your praying mantis well cared for and happy, you'll basically have a cool little alien just chilling in your house.

🍄 **Stick insects:** Another fascinating but low-maintenance insect pet is the stick insect. Their habitat requirements are the same as for praying mantises, and they largely eat lettuce. Imagine having a living twig as a pet—what's more goblincore than that? It's worth noting that if these insects escape your enclosure, they can wreak ecological havoc on the environment, so make sure their habitat is well sealed.

🍄 **Field crickets:** These musical insects make great pets, as long as you like the sound of their chirping. Their habitat requirements are the same as those of the previous bugs, and they like to eat lettuce and fruit. Having one of these guys as a pet means you always get to fall asleep to the soothing sound of crickets.

The Care and Keeping of Creatures

If you've decided you not only relate to scaly and slimy friends but you also want to keep one as a pet, here's some info on how best to keep your goblin pet happy.

This section isn't going to be the be-all and end-all guide to keeping reptiles and amphibians, but it's a good starting point so you can start to visualize what it would be like to have a slimy little familiar living in your room. Do you have the basic items needed to care for this pet? Do you know where to find the items you don't have? Do you have time and space and enough mental bandwidth to care for a creature who might live for years? These are some things to consider as you read through this section. (After you've committed to the idea, you should do more research, and maybe even talk to other people who own the same kind of pet, before you bring an animal into your home.)

Maybe you'll start out interested in lizards but come to the realization that you're better suited for a hermit crab. That's okay! It's great that you're seriously considering what pet you could best take care of. After all, even though these pets are a little more unique than a cat or a dog, they still require lots of thought and care. If, for whatever reason, you can't meet an animal's basic needs, that animal isn't for you. Consider this section a starting guide to see which creature is best suited to you, or if you're better off collecting frog stuffed animals.

FROGS

LIFESPAN: Depending on the species, frogs can live anywhere from 3 to 15 years.

HABITAT: Since some frogs are totally aquatic, some are terrestrial, and some prefer trees, you'll have to consider the needs of your particular frog species when creating their habitat. Here's some good rules of thumb, though:

- Aquatic frogs: For these frogs, you'll need a true aquarium, not just a terrarium. Make sure you can accommodate an aquarium of at least 10 gallons, that you can keep the aquarium water clean and fresh and free of chlorine, and that the water remains at the proper temperature for your frog (probably at least 77 degrees Fahrenheit).

- Terrestrial frogs: Most terrestrial frogs will require at least a 10-gallon terrarium, although the terrarium won't be as deep as the aquatic frog's aquarium. In most terrariums, you'll want to make sure there's a bowl of water for the frog to soak in, and a basking lamp or heating pad, and a spray bottle to mist the tank to ensure the enclosure remains at the proper temperature and humidity. Make sure to put a lid on the terrarium so the frogs can't hop out!

- Arboreal frogs: If you decide to adopt a tree frog, you'll need a special terrarium that's taller than it is wide, with room to add plants, branches, and vines for your frogs to hide in. Your terrarium should be at least 15 gallons. Again, you'll need a basking lamp or heating pad, and a spray bottle to mist the tank to ensure that the temperature and humidity stay consistent, and you'll need a bowl of water for the frogs to soak in.

DIET: Most frogs eat a variety of insects in the wild, but in captivity it can be difficult to give your frog enough variety for them to get all the nutrients they need. Because of this, no matter what you feed your frog, it's important to dust the food with nutrient supplements before feeding. This ensures that your frog will get all the nutrition it needs to be healthy. Also, make sure you keep an eye on portion sizes. Like many animals, frogs will keep eating until they get sick, so it's up to you to make sure they don't overeat.

HEALTH: Don't plan on cuddling with your frog, since they don't respond well to being held often. The oils, soaps, and lotions on your hands can upset a frog's skin, plus some frogs carry salmonella. If you're picking up a frog, it's best to use latex gloves and wash your hands after.

ETC.: There are a lot of different frog species that flourish in captivity, so make sure to do your research before heading to the pet store or pet rescue.

LIZARDS

LIFESPAN: Lizards live for 5 to 50 years (yes, really).

HABITAT: There are lots of different lizards with different habitat needs, so make sure to research your particular lizard when you're building them a home. That said, lizards will pretty much always need a heating light and a full-spectrum light to keep their temperature consistent and healthy. Most terrestrial lizards will need a vivarium, which is like an aquarium or a terrarium, except it's specifically for cold-blooded animals. Lizards will also need branches, sand, tree bark, peat moss, or other environmental items to make their enclosure mimic their natural habitat and give them places to hide and climb. Different species of lizards can grow to be different sizes, so make sure you take your specific lizard's average adult size into account when setting up their habitat. You'll want plenty of room for the adult lizard to move around inside the vivarium.

DIET: Different lizards have different dietary needs. For example, some lizards can get by with mostly commercial lizard food, while others need live prey. Some lizards can eat a small amount of fruits and vegetables and others will need to eat primarily ants. As with frogs, you'll probably need to supplement your lizard's diet with certain vitamins and minerals to keep them healthy. Make sure you're able to feed your lizard according to its particular dietary needs.

HEALTH: Keep your lizard's vivarium clean, warm, and safe, and make sure that it has appropriate enrichment activities without being too crowded. A lot of seemingly insignificant things can make lizards sick. For example, if the humidity in your lizard's tank isn't high enough, it can have trouble shedding, and if your lizard isn't getting enough calcium, it can develop bone disease.

ETC.: If you want to keep more than one lizard in a single tank, do your research about which types of lizards do well with companions and which ones don't. Lizards who live together might also have a higher risk of some infections, so keep that in mind too.

HERMIT CRABS

LIFESPAN: Hermit crabs can live more than 10 years with proper care.

HABITAT: Hermit crabs are social and should live in groups of two or more, and they need at least a 10-gallon glass tank per two hermit crabs. For substrate, make sure there's at least 3 inches of sand, or sand mixed with coconut fibers, covering the bottom of the tank. Hermit crabs love to dig! They also require two water bowls, one with freshwater and one with salt water. Make sure there's enough water in the bowls for the crabs to submerge themselves, but not so much that they drown. To keep your hermit crab cage warm and humid, get a heat lamp that will keep the cage between 70 and 80 degrees Fahrenheit and mist your crabs with dechlorinated water daily. Don't forget to mist, otherwise your crabs will suffocate! Finally, be sure to include some places for your hermit crabs to hide and climb, such as driftwood, hollow branches, plastic plants, caves, and shells.

DIET: Hermit crabs are omnivores, so it's good to feed them a mix of things. Hermit crab food is easy to buy at pet food stores, but you can also supplement their diet with lettuce, spinach, papaya, mangoes, seaweed, carrots, and nuts. It's also a good idea to include a calcium supplement to support their shells and exoskeletons.

HEALTH: Hermit crabs regularly molt their exoskeleton. When doing this, they bury themselves under their substrate and shouldn't be disturbed at all until the process is over. It can be good to have a second tank to hold your other hermit crab(s) during this time, so that they don't interrupt the molting. The crabs might also fight over the shed exoskeleton after the molting is done, which is another good reason for the two-tank method. Make sure to keep your molting hermit crab humid and well misted, since this will help the process a lot.

ETC.: Your hermit crab will need a new, larger shell every so often. When one of your hermit crabs sheds its shell, make sure you get another, slightly bigger shell for it to move into.

Communing with Creatures

If you read the last section and thought, "Wow, I am not prepared to keep any of these animals as pets," that's fine. Actually, it's great! It's important to be honest with yourself, especially when it comes to your ability to provide care to a living thing. However, just because you're not about to go out and adopt a pet frog doesn't mean you can't find other ways to feel close to your amphibian friends. There are lots of ways to celebrate animals without keeping them as pets, and goblins are big fans of celebrating the weird and wild without needing to tame or domesticate. Your goblin familiar doesn't need to physically exist in your space in order to exist in your heart. Here are some ways to bring your favorite creature into your life without literally bringing one into your lair.

STUFFED ANIMALS: This feels like the obvious fix. There are tons of stuffed animals in so many different, cool styles. No matter what aesthetic, you can likely find a plush of your favorite animal that suits you. Plus, a lot of the more goblin-friendly animals aren't exactly cuddle-friendly in real life. If you want to cuddle a frog, you're going to have a much better time snuggling with your plush frog than with a real one (and real frogs everywhere will be grateful that you're not trying to cuddle them). You could even make your own plush goblin friend if you wanted to! Stuffed animals are a great way to feel close to the animal you love without literally needing to be close to that animal.

ACCESSORIES: If you're the kind of goblin who likes to wear their heart on their literal sleeve, this is a great option. Represent your love of sweet, slimy creatures with everything from purses to hair clips to manicures to jewelry. Whether you style yourself simply or you like to go all out with your outfits, you can find a level of animal accessories that works for you. If you love snakes, get a pair of socks with snakes printed on them, make some earrings with cool clay snakes, or paint snakes on your nails to show off your love to the world—or do all these things at once! There's nothing wrong with dressing to show off your passions, and wearing your favorite animal every day might even make you feel more comfortable and confident. Embrace the power of weird accessories!

ART: Share your love of your favorite creature by making them into art! Whether you prefer painting, embroidery, papier-mâché, wood carving, or just doodling in your free time, making art of something you love is guaranteed to make you feel closer to that thing. You get to spend time thinking about turtles and looking at reference photos of turtles and then making art that represents what turtles mean to you (it's turtles all the way down). Plus, it's a great way to share your love with the world. If you get tired of drawing turtles by yourself, try hosting a craft night and challenging your friends to draw turtles or encouraging them to draw their own favorite animal. Art is a great way to create community and share your talents.

DECOR: Much like accessorizing your outfit, decorating is a great way to surround yourself with reminders of the things you love. Whether you make or buy or thrift your decor, filling your lair with reminders of your favorite goblin creature is a quick way to make your space feel like home. You could hang up posters of lizards, find pillows with frogs on them, get a bedspread with cute cartoon crabs, or even make a snake-themed gallery wall. When your friends come over for a creature craft night, you can ask them to each make art of their favorite animal that you can display in your space. That way, your decor will remind you of both your favorite goblin creatures and your best goblin friends. There are so many ways to bring your interests into your space, and even if you can't have a pet, you can still fill your lair with love.

TATTOOS: Getting a tattoo of your favorite creature is a commitment, but depending on what kind of goblin you are, it might be a commitment you're ready for. What better way to show off your love for amphibians than by getting a tattoo of one on your body? Tattoos will show your commitment to your favorite animal, and they'll definitely make you feel closer to that animal as well. After all, how much closer could something be than on your skin? Tattoos also allow you to add some flair to your favorite creature. You could get a tattoo of a frog driving a boat, a snail wearing a fancy hat, or a turtle with a bouquet of flowers peeking out of its shell. Depending on what kind of art you and your tattoo artist come up with, your tattoo can portray all kinds of things about your favorite animal.

TIME OUTSIDE: The good old-fashioned way of connecting with the world is a classic for a reason. Whether you decide to go for a walk around your neighborhood, take a hike through a forest, or wander through a museum or library, there are all kinds of ways you can see, learn about, and connect with your favorite creatures. Checking out nearby streams for tadpoles could be a great way to feel close to frogs, even if you can't have them in your house. Researching snakes and turtles at the library gives you a chance to get to know these creatures better, even if you don't feel ready to keep one under your roof. You don't have to own an animal to feel close to that animal—in fact, that's a pretty capitalist idea when you think about it. Appreciating the animal from a distance, in its natural habitat, can make you feel just as connected to that animal as keeping one in your room would. There's so much more to see when you get to witness an animal in its natural habitat, too. We can feel close to the things we love without needing to be physically close to them at all times.

Creatures are all around us—creeping along the pavement, scuttling under rocks, dozing in the dirt. We don't always notice them, but they're always there. When we realize how common these little animals are, we can also acknowledge that they're already a big part of our lives. Maybe there's a family of frogs in your yard who start singing every night when the sun goes down, or maybe you spent an afternoon one day watching a snail slime across the sidewalk. These may seem like minor details, but actually they're proof of how entwined our lives are with the creatures around us. Would it still feel like nighttime if you couldn't hear those frogs? Would your afternoon have been lonely without that snail?

The more we notice these often-ignored animals, the more we can begin to learn from them. Start paying attention to turtles when you walk past your local pond or watch the hermit crabs next time you're at the beach. Slow down. Notice what you didn't notice last time you saw that animal. Stay curious, and you're sure to learn so much more from these weird creatures than you ever thought you could.

The more you pay attention, the more you'll see that every creature has its own personality and its own quirks. No two lizards follow the exact same path up a tree, no two snails will eat a cabbage leaf at the same speed. The variations may be slight, but they're there if you pay attention. And the more you see these differences, the more you'll appreciate each creature for the individual being that it is. There's never been a hermit crab exactly like the one you found in that tide pool last week, and there never will be again. To live in a world filled with strange, slimy, crunchy, cold-blooded creatures is to live in a world full of strange, slimy, crunchy, cold-blooded miracles. Not everyone sees this, but goblins take pride in the knowledge that we get to live among snails.

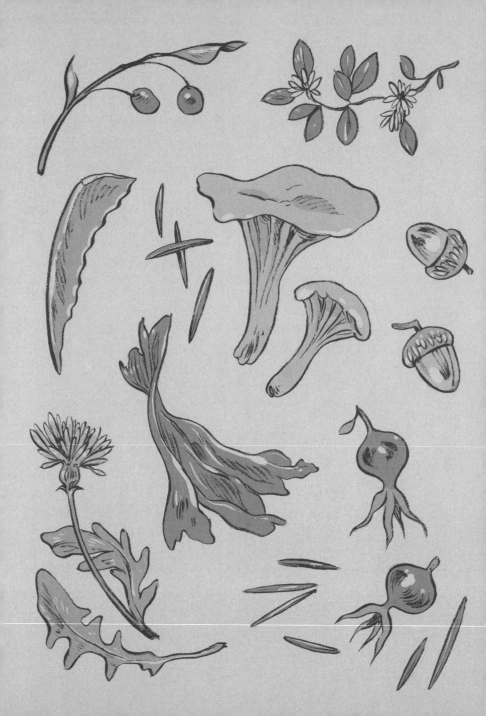

CHAPTER 6

The Goblin Market

Turning foraged goods into
potions and treats

Looking for a wonderful, goblin-friendly way to get in touch with nature and learn about the environment you live in? Look no further than foraging! Foraging is searching for and collecting food in the wild. Rather than go to the grocery store to get chives, for instance, you can do some research to see if there could be any wild onions growing near you. This is a great way to discover your local flora and get a deeper understanding of the ecosystem surrounding you. When you start paying attention to which flowers are in bloom and which herbs grow in different biomes, you'll begin to see patterns in the ways that nature works, and things that may have once seemed mysterious will suddenly become familiar.

Whether you live in a rural area or an urban one, there are ways to work foraging into your life. From visiting the woods to look for useful greens to planting your own, there's no one way to forage. Foraging is perfect for the goblin lifestyle, since it incorporates so many different goblin traits. It can be a great way to get out in nature and learn more about the natural world, it's free and accessible, it's a fun way to get your hands dirty, it can help you become more self-sufficient, and it's a natural extension of collecting and sharing cool treasures. Foraging is basically picking up a cool leaf and putting it in your pocket, except that the leaf is basil or thyme, or maybe rose hip or lavender, and your pocket is your pantry.

Foraging can also be a great addition to grocery shopping. Sure, you might not have time or space to grow *all* your food in your apartment, but it can be nice to supplement the foods you buy with food you grow or find on your own. Not only can foraging cut down on your grocery bill, but you're less likely to be exposed to the pesticides that can be found on commercially grown greens. Plus, there's going to be less packaging waste if you're growing food for yourself or finding food that's naturally out growing in nature. If nothing else, food you pick yourself is always going to taste a little better than food you buy. Again, no one is expecting you to start a farm in your backyard, but it's amazing the difference that even a small amount of foraging can make!

Perhaps the biggest benefit of foraging, though, is the connection it fosters between goblins and their environment. It's easy to feel disconnected from nature if you live in an urban or even suburban area. Foraging reminds you that nature is all around you, and you can connect to it much more easily than you might have thought. Bringing herb and veggie plants into your space, learning about which plants around you are secretly edible, and cooking with food you grew and found by yourself are all great ways to restore your relationship to the natural world. The more you forage, the more you'll learn about your environment, and the stronger your bond to nature will become. You're part of the natural world, and foraging will help you see this connection and understand the balance and ecosystems that surround us all.

How to Forage in Woods and Green Spaces

So, you live near the woods or a green space, and you want to start taking advantage of the great foraging opportunities presented to you. Great! With just a little prep and planning, it's easy to start foraging. It's good to do a bit of groundwork ahead of time so that you know exactly what you're looking for. You also don't want to go out and pick a thousand dandelions if you only need five! Leave some dandelions for the rest of the people and animals and bugs that need them. Don't be wasteful when foraging, just take what you need. Make a game plan before you go so that you can forage in a way that's most thoughtful toward both your needs and the needs of your environment. Following are a few ways to get good at foraging.

- **Find out what edible plants are available near you.** In order to find edible plants in your area, try checking online, at the library, or at a local botanical garden or greenhouse. Your botanical garden or other pro-plant space might even offer classes on how to forage locally and what to look for!

- **Bring a guidebook.** It's always a good idea to bring some kind of guide to local edible flora with you when you forage, since lots of flowers and berries and greens look similar to each other. If you can, maybe even find an expert who's willing to show you the foraging ropes the first time or two that you try it. Remember to be very careful of poisonous plants and their nonpoisonous lookalikes!

- **Dress to forage.** It can be tempting to embrace the romance of dressing like a renaissance fair rogue to go collect your natural spoils, but you're going to be a lot better off if you wear comfortable shoes and clothes you can move in. You don't want to get mud on your homemade scabbard, after all. If you head out foraging, wear clothes that allow a good range of movement while also protecting you from the elements.

- **Find out what to avoid.** Look up the various dangers that might exist in a forest near you. This could mean ticks, snakes, moose, mosquitos, or even aggressively thorny or otherwise painful plants. Spend enough time researching that you can recognize these dangers on sight. Make sure you take the necessary precautions too, if there are any (i.e., not leaving skin exposed for ticks, making noise as you move through the woods to scare off moose or deer).

- **Bring the proper tools.** There are plenty of specialized tools you can use when foraging—for instance, berry pickers: metal claws that you can rake through a bush to scoop up all the berries. If they make your life easier, embrace them all! But likely the only things you'll need when foraging are your foraging guidebook, something to hold your finds, and, of course, your foraging-friendly outfit. For holding what you forage, you can use a bucket, an old grocery bag, a lunch box, a bowl— basically anything that you don't mind getting a little dirty and carrying for a while. (Or see page 154 for instructions on how to make your own container.)

- **Steer clear of mushrooms.** This book is not going to tell you how to forage for mushrooms, nor will it encourage you to do so. There are just too many risks! Even if you have a great mushroom guidebook, there are many mushrooms that look extremely similar, and some are really dangerous. If you're a mushroom amateur, consider growing your own instead of searching for mushrooms in the wild. (You can grow them on a cool-looking old log in your kitchen, so they're also decor!) If you absolutely insist on foraging for mushrooms, bring your finds to your local botanical garden or other botanical experts to have them assessed. It doesn't hurt to have a second set of eyes on your shrooms, especially if you're an amateur and the other eyes are a professional. Long story short: unless you're a fungus expert, don't pick wild mushrooms. Grow your own instead! (And if you are a fungus expert, congratulations on your life choices that led you to such a cool career.)

A QUICK AND EASY FORAGING CONTAINER

If you're going to be foraging a lot, try making this container. It is incredibly easy to make and will last you years. It's also made from recycled materials, which is a big goblin plus. Fill it with berries or greens, rinse it out, and use it over and over to carry all your treasures while you're out foraging!

WHAT YOU'LL NEED

- ★ A marker
- ★ An empty plastic milk jug
- ★ Scissors or a box cutter
- ★ About 2 feet of cord (thin rope)
- ★ Paint, stickers, or other decorations (optional)

WHAT TO DO

1. Use your marker to draw an angled line from just above the top of the milk jug handle to about a third or half of the way down the front of the jug. Draw the same line on the other side of the jug, and connect the lines in the front of the jug.

2. Using your scissors or box cutter, cut along the lines you drew.

3. Wrap the cord around your waist and tie one half around the other in an overhand knot. (Check "Threading a needle" on page 76 for an explanation of how to do an overhand knot.)

4. Tie the other end of the cord around the handle of your milk jug. You want the cord to rest around your waist, so make sure the cord is tight enough to do so but not so tight as to be uncomfortable.

5. Cut the cord to a shorter length if it's too long.

6. If you want, decorate your container by drawing or painting on it or adding stickers. (Paint or markers may eventually rub or flake off, but that just means you can decorate it again.)

7. You're done! Now you've got a container that will stay attached to you without making you use your hands, and it'll hold plenty of foraged goods.

Nine Plants You Didn't Know You Could Eat

If you're ever looking for a special, natural something to add to your favorite recipe, you don't have to look any further than your backyard. There are tons of edible plants out there, and you probably never realized that lots of the plants growing in your garden, or in the woods nearby, are actually edible. Whether you're looking to make tea or jam, or add some unexpected flavor and color to your favorite dish, you're likely to find just what you need right outside your door, no trip to the grocery store required. That's the power of foraging!

Before we get into these magical, edible plants, it's once again important to note that you want to be careful when foraging for plants that you plan to eat. Lots of safe plants have toxic doppelgängers. You don't want to make yourself (or your friends) sick, so make sure to keep a good guidebook with you, and again consider showing your foraged finds to an expert before you eat them. Also keep in mind that, just like regular produce from the grocery store, you never know what you might end up being allergic to. Finally, note that soil toxicity and potential exposure to pesticides can change a delicious plant into a dangerous one. Keep all this in mind while you forage, and you'll be one safe, happy goblin with a full pantry.

- **Kelp**: Seaweed is a popular snack, of course, but you may not have considered that kelp is also edible. (Okay, maybe you did if you eat a lot of Chinese, Japanese, or Korean food. But what's common knowledge to one person might be totally new to another, and this list celebrates that fact.) If you live near the coast, try fishing a piece of sugar kelp out of the water—you can cut it up and eat every part! Kelp is good dried, but it can also be pickled, made into pasta, added to salads, and much more. It's incredibly nutrient rich, and it's great for the environment too. What can't kelp do?

- **Stinging nettle**: Although you'll want to be careful when foraging for nettles (they sting, hence the name), this plant has lots of culinary applications. You'll want to wear gloves while handling the nettles initially, but once they've been exposed to heat they'll be safe to handle. From there, you can turn  the leaves and vines into a salad or pizza topping, or you can even use them as the main ingredient in pesto. Stinging nettles make a particularly unexpected and rewarding foraged food.

- **Cattails**: Cattails are a plant that you'll have to catch at a specific time in their growth cycle, because you want to avoid eating a mouthful of cattail fluff (or at least, you *probably* want to avoid eating a mouthful of cattail fluff—the choice is ultimately up to you). If you harvest cattails while the catkins are still green, you can eat them cooked or raw, and even cook them up like corn on the cob. The roots and pollen can also be used in recipes, making the cattail yet another deliciously diverse plant.

- **Wild rose:** Wild roses are as tasty as they are beautiful, which is saying a lot, because they're really beautiful. In late fall, rose plants bear a fruit called rose hip that has a light, citrusy taste. Rose hips can be used to make jelly, drinks, or tea, and they provide a nice fruity flavor at a time of year when there isn't much fruity flavor to be had elsewhere. And of course, the blossoms of wild roses can also be used to add a stunning pink color to many foods, if you want to cook something pretty.

- **Fiddlehead ferns:** These unique, curly greens form at the tops of ostrich ferns for just a few weeks a year, so if you want to forage for them, make sure to mark your calendar! Fiddleheads can be sauteed to make a sweet, nutty vegetable side to any meal. You can also roast them, fry them, throw them in a salad, marinate them . . . the options are endless (and delicious). Make sure you don't eat them raw, though! Ostrich ferns can cause food poisoning if consumed raw. If you're foraging for your own fiddleheads, make sure you stick to ostrich ferns, as other varieties can be toxic.

- **Milk thistle:** Don't be fooled into thinking that milk thistle is just a pretty purple flower. It can also be made into a delicious snack, and it's been used for centuries as a tonic for bad livers. Not every flower has that much power! Most parts of the milk thistle can be eaten, from the flower bulb to the leaves to the stalk, but it's the seeds of this plant that have the most applications. Toast the seeds and eat them as a snack, or grind them up to make them into a seasoning or even a coffee substitute.

- **Pine needles:** Yes, it's true—pine needles are edible! You probably don't want to chomp down on a tree branch, but pine needles can be steeped in cream or simple syrup to add some sweet, spicy, pine-infused flavor to your food. Use your pine syrup or pine cream in desserts to upgrade a regular sweet treat to something really special. (What could be more goblin-y than dessert flavored with foraged pine needles?)

- **Meadowsweet:** Anything elderflower can do, meadowsweet can do better. This ancient herb was once highly sought after for its medicinal effects, but now it's more likely to be found as a sweet, flavorful addition to cordials, meads, and teas. If you want to make your friends a truly memorable cocktail, try infusing simple syrup with meadowsweet or simply making your own cordial with this fragrant flower.

- **Tree bark:** Lots of tree bark is edible, as long as you're harvesting the inner bark and not the coarse outer bark. Bark should be harvested carefully, as taking a tree's bark can damage the tree. As long as you're careful and take the right bark, though, you'll have a great foraged treasure! Tree bark can be used to make tea, ground into flour, made into an oil or a salve, or even sliced into strips and boiled to make a forager-friendly pasta. Make sure you look into edible types of tree bark before you harvest, though, or the tree's bark will definitely be worse than its bite.

ACORN BRITTLE

If you're ready to put your foraging abilities to the test, start by making acorn brittle with the acorns you harvested. It's fun and easy to do, and it'll have all your friends saying, "Wait, you made this with *acorns*?!"

WHAT YOU'LL NEED

- ★ 1–1¼ cups acorn nutmeats
- ★ 1–1¼ cups superfine sugar (granulated sugar can also work if that's what you have around)
- ★ A towel
- ★ A hammer or mallet
- ★ A pot large enough to hold all your acorns
- ★ A saucepan
- ★ A baking tray lined with parchment paper

WHAT TO DO

1. First, go through your acorns and throw out the ones that aren't good. Good acorns look and feel good—they're a little heavy and look clean and polished. Bad acorns might be too light, too small, discolored, dull, or full of weevil holes. Toss your bad acorns (ideally outside or in a compost bin) and keep the good ones.

2. Lay down a towel on a sturdy surface and spread a handful of acorns on top, then fold half of the towel over the acorns. Then, take your hammer or mallet and start smashing hard enough to crack the shells off the acorns. Once you're done, collect your nutmeats (sorry, that's what they're called), discard your shells, and do the process again until you've shelled 1–1¼ cups.

3. Leach the acorns. This is crucial to get rid of tannins that taste bitter and could leave you feeling sick. Fill a pot with acorns and water, then bring to a boil. Once the water boils, pour it out and refill the pot with fresh water, and then boil it again. Keep doing this until the water is clear.

4. Pour your sugar into your saucepan, and heat it over low heat, stirring constantly. Sugar burns easily, so this is a process you want to keep a close eye on. Make sure you don't get any hot sugar on your skin.

5. Once the sugar melts and turns a dark brown, pour in your acorns and continue to stir until the acorns are fully incorporated into the sugar.

6. Take your saucepan off the heat and *carefully* pour the mixture onto the baking tray lined with parchment paper. Use your spoon or a spatula to spread the mixture around so it's evenly distributed on the tray.

7. Leave the tray to cool. Once the mixture has hardened, you're done.

Your Wild Medicine Cabinet

If you're looking for something even more useful than your average plant, you're in luck. There are plenty of plants in the wild that serve medicinal purposes and can offer a bit of natural pain relief, treat skin conditions, relieve nausea, and do many other things as well. Are they as potent as something you could get prescribed, or even over the counter? No, but if you prefer to treat mild maladies the natural way, these plants can definitely help. Sometimes it's just fun to know which weeds can offer headache relief, too. Everyone loves feeling a little witchy.

> Did you know that there are many types of plants that have historically been used as abortifacients? In the past, pregnant people used all kinds of plants to help induce abortion. It's almost as though abortion is as natural as the plants themselves.

Keep in mind that the types of medicinal plants that grow near you can differ from the ones listed below, since different plants grow in different places (who would've thought!). Although there are different biomes covered here, the specific plants available in your area can still differ, and there are definitely way more medicinal plants growing near you than we could ever exhaustively list here, anyway. Do some research on your local flora before you start foraging for these types of plants! It's a great way to get connected with your plant neighbors and general plant community.

Another important note here: these plants are great, but they won't replace the marvels of modern medicine. If you have a serious illness, don't substitute natural remedies for your prescribed medication. Also, if you want to start using any of these plant remedies regularly, talk to your doctor first about how they might affect your body or interact with your other medications. Just because these plants are natural doesn't mean they won't have any negative effects. Finally, consider any allergies you might have before you dive into the world of medicinal plants. It would suck to whip up a cure-all tea and end up with hives.

- **Aloe vera**: This desert plant is popular for its burn-treatment abilities. Cut off a small piece of aloe leaf and rub the aloe gel inside on a burn, or rub the gel on a sunburn a few times per day, and your burn will be feeling better in no time.

- **Turmeric**: Turmeric root is well-known for its anti-inflammatory properties and for its antioxidants when used as an ingredient. Making tea from turmeric root is an easy and delicious way to get the anti-inflammatory benefits of this plant. Fermenting turmeric will make its effects even more potent, and fermented turmeric is thought to improve liver function.

- **Chamomile**: Another medicinal plant that makes great tea! Chamomile can be used to treat sleeplessness and mild anxiety symptoms, since it generally has a calming, drowsiness-inducing effect. Making a cup of chamomile tea before bed will likely help you sleep better.

- **Feverfew**: This pretty flower has been used for hundreds of years to treat headaches. Consuming any part of the plant above the root can offer headache and migraine relief, although taking feverfew regularly and then stopping suddenly can cause headaches to return. Drying this plant and using the leaves to make tea is a calming way to treat a headache.

- **Ginger**: Ginger isn't just delicious, it's also very useful as an anti-nausea treatment. Whether you're dealing with motion sickness, morning sickness, or sickness related to a medical treatment, ginger can offer some relief. Take ginger raw, dried, as tea—there are lots of ways to work a bit of medicinal ginger into your day to help with nausea.

- **Yarrow**: This plant is a bit of a cure-all, as it's been used both internally and externally to help with everything from toothaches to fevers to diarrhea to healing wounds. Almost every part of this plant can be used to heal something. You can take yarrow dried, as tea, or as a poultice on a cut. This ancient plant has a lot to offer.

A City Goblin's Foraging Guide

Maybe you've been reading this chapter and thinking, "This all seems cool, but I live in the city! Can I still forage if I don't have much access to green space?" Don't worry, sweet city goblin, you can still forage to your heart's content—but your style of foraging and the treasures you find might look a little different.

For city goblins, foraging might involve more kitchen-counter gardens, or making use of small balconies as spaces for growing small selections of food. It might also look like keeping a reusable grocery bag with you at all times, just in case you happen upon something to forage during your commute. City foraging involves a little more creativity, but that doesn't mean it can't be done. In fact, goblins are ideal city foragers since they love to get creative and keep an eye out for cool stuff. After all, what is foraging if not treasure hunting?

In this section, you'll find lots of ideas for foraging (and growing) plants in the city. If you don't have access to green space, create your own! If you want readily available fresh food, grow it in your apartment! If you like to go out and find unexpectedly edible plants, you can do that too. City goblins are just as capable of foraging as any other type of goblin.

GOING GREEN:
HOW TO ACCESS GREEN SPACE

Unfortunately, we live in a capitalist society. This means that access to green space can be severely limited based on income, geography, environmental racism, and other factors that mostly boil down to money. (Environmental racism means the ways in which environmental policy and infrastructure problems disproportionately harm Black people, Indigenous people, and other people of color—like how Flint, Michigan, a primarily Black community, was left without drinkable water for years.) Because of this, lots of people who live in cities have pretty negligible access to greenery, which sucks for a lot of reasons, but for our purposes it sucks because it limits your foraging abilities.

However, there are ways to create more green space near you. Here are some ideas for how to improve your life by improving your access to nature.

Join or start a community garden. Before you decide to create your own community garden, do some research and find out if there's already a community garden active near you. There's no need to start your own garden if your area already has a perfectly good one nearby! If you can't find any local community gardens, you can consider making one. Starting a community garden isn't an easy thing to do, but if you have the time and resources, it can be a great addition to your area. This won't be an overnight process, and it'll take work—you'll need to gauge community interest; hold meetings for interested people; find sponsors; look into local laws about renting or buying garden space; choose, buy, and prepare a site; and probably way more. But if you can do it, go for it!

> If you can't find a way to make your community garden free for everyone who uses it, then don't make one! These gardens are a great way to combat food insecurity and increase the sense of community in an area, but if people have to pay to use your garden, you're not really offering any of these things. You're just creating more private land.

Turn your apartment into a greenhouse. Look into plants that grow well indoors, and start keeping your own greenery on your windowsill, on your kitchen counter, or on your balcony. Whether you want to stay small and grow a few herbs or go big and try something like tomatoes or lemons, there are plenty of plants that will flourish indoors. If your thumb isn't exactly green, start with something easy to grow (and hard to kill) like mint or a calamansi tree. And yes, it counts as foraging if you grew the food you're foraging for!

Visit public parks. You might not have considered the foraging potential of your local park before. A walk through the park can yield acorns, dandelions, wild roses, and maybe even cattails—all edible plants that you can forage without leaving the city. Keep an eye out next time you go to the park for a walk or a picnic, and you might find more to forage than you expected. Make sure to look up local regulations about foraging in public parks before you dig in, though!

Check out decorative greenery. Most urban planners are sure to include a handful of trees, shrubs, or flowers when they're organizing a city. Even if there isn't a park near you, there might be a street with a row of trees or bushes. Rather than disregard this greenery as purely aesthetic, take some time to identify exactly what types of plants they are. Although they were planted for decorative purposes, these plants might also be great for foraging.

Although it's sort of a gray area legally, guerilla grafting is an inventive and interesting way that some people in cities are combating food insecurity. Guerilla grafting is a process in which people graft branches of fruit- and nut-bearing trees to existing, inedible trees in cities. This means that the existing trees will begin to bear food on their newly grafted branches.

A GARDEN? INDOORS? IT'S MORE LIKELY THAN YOU THINK

So you want to turn your apartment into your own personal foraging haven, but you're not sure where to start. Don't worry, because no matter your gardening skill level, there's a great indoor plant for you. Whether you're a gardening genius or a newbie, the following plants are great contenders for growing at home. And once you've got everything planted, you can forage to your heart's content without ever leaving your lair!

- **Any herb:** If you're just getting started, herbs are a great choice for your apartment garden. They're hardy, fast growing, and easy to care for, and there's no better addition to your meal than some fresh-picked herbs. Try growing thyme, basil, mint, rosemary, parsley, oregano . . . the list goes on. As a bonus, growing herbs will make your apartment smell great.

- **Oyster mushrooms:** While there are a handful of mushrooms that are easy to grow indoors, oyster mushrooms are particularly simple (and delicious). You can keep them in a warm, damp, dark place (under your sink is great!), and they can grow on anything from straw to coffee grounds. If you're new to growing mushrooms and nervous about the process, you can also buy a mushroom growing kit that'll give you everything you need to grow happy fungi.

- **Lemon balm:** If you're looking for simple, medicinal plants to keep inside, lemon balm is a great option. It's as easy to grow as any herb, but it has the added benefit of being good for your digestive system. If you're someone who gets a lot of stomach aches, this is a great, easy plant to keep in your home.

- **Microgreens:** These tiny sprouts pack a big punch of vitamins and minerals, and they're easy to grow indoors. They grow well, even in low light, and they don't need a lot of upkeep. All you need is some space on your windowsill, and you could be sprouting and harvesting microgreens in no time!

- **Lavender:** This flower serves double duty as both an edible plant and a medicinal one. You can dry lavender flowers to add a floral flavor to your drinks and desserts or put them in your bath to soothe muscle pain. Lavender oil can also be used topically to help with wounds and skin conditions or inhaled for a calming effect. That's a lot of benefits from a plant that you can grow in your kitchen!

EDIBLE PLANTS IN URBAN AREAS

You might be surprised at how many common plants are edible—you'll probably find that you pass by more than one of these edible plants on your commute. Once you learn which weeds, trees, and flowers are ripe for foraging, you'll start to see your city in a whole new light. Rather than being a cold, gray, unnatural place, a city can become an unexpected haven for clever foragers who know what to look for. Just because a city doesn't have the same green space as a suburb or a rural area doesn't mean you can't indulge your goblin side and become a master forager (as long as you're foraging in public spaces and not your neighbors' yards). Happy hunting!

- **Dandelions**: You probably spent a lot of time as a kid either pulling up dandelions, making dandelion flower crowns, or blowing dandelion seeds to make wishes. But did you know that dandelions can actually make a delicious, nutritious food? You can steep the roots into a tea, toss the greens in a salad, ferment the flowers into a wine, and so much more. With this much flexibility, you'll never look at dandelions as weeds again. Dandelions can be found all throughout North America, as well as Australia, New Zealand, India, southern Africa, and parts of Europe.

- **Clover**: Not only are clovers a pretty ground covering, but the blossoms can add a light, sweet, and floral taste to teas, jellies, syrups, drinks, and more. Simmer the blossoms with some water and use the resulting reduction in anything you want. Red clover can even be dried and ground into flour! Who would have thought these little flowers had so much potential? Clover can be found almost everywhere, except southeast Asia and Australia.

- **Chickweed**: This so-called weed is easy to find and contains a huge amount of nutrients—proof that weeds are a forager's best friend. The leaves and flowers of this plant are edible and can be eaten raw or cooked. Try adding them to salads, soups, pastas, pestos, and more for a nutrient boost. Chickweed can be found in the continental US, Europe, and parts of Asia. Note that in some parts of the US this plant is considered invasive, so by foraging for it you're actually doing the environment a favor!

- **Curly dock**: You've probably seen this plant before, since it grows basically everywhere. Maybe you spotted it on the side of the road, or in a park, or growing between sidewalk cracks. But curly dock isn't just widespread, it's also edible. Forage for this plant in the late spring and early summer, and you can peel and cook up the stems like any other vegetable. Curly dock has a light sour flavor and can be eaten raw or cooked (or even pickled). It's the ideal plant for city foragers! Curly dock can be found in the continental US, Europe, Asia, and nearly all of Canada.

- **Acorns**: Why do we celebrate the almond but ignore the readily available, and extremely vitamin-rich, acorn? Acorns are a nut like any other, and if they're prepared correctly (they'll need to be leached to remove the bitter tannins—there are instructions for this on page 161), you can use them to cook all kinds of dishes. Roasted acorns make a delicious snack or a great addition to baked goods, and acorn flour is popular for its nutty flavor. Oak trees can be found in most of the continental US and Canada, Asia, Europe, northern Africa, and Central and South America.

- **Broadleaf plantain**: These weeds are everywhere, which is great news for foragers. Broadleaf plantain leaves can be eaten raw or cooked, but you'll want to make sure you harvest them in the spring when the leaves are young, or they'll become stringy and bitter and generally less appetizing. Once you harvest some of these leaves, try subbing them into recipes that normally call for spinach. You're sure to be happy with the results.

Broadleaf plantains can be found in most of North America, Asia, and Europe.

- **Hackberry:** Hackberry trees are often planted around cities as decorative foliage, but the goblin forager should note that their value goes beyond the aesthetic. These berries have a thin skin surrounding an edible, incredibly nutrient-rich seed at the center. They make a crunchy, nutty snack with a slightly sweet taste. Harvest the berries during the winter and you'll have a delicious snack or a fun new ingredient to try (hackberries can be used to make nut milk!). Hackberry trees can be found across most of North America.

- **Lamb's-quarter:** Found all over the world, lamb's-quarter is a popular and even sought-after food in many countries. Lucky for city goblins, it's easy to find and harvest. The leaves and flowers of this plant are edible, although it's more common to eat the leaves. If you want to cook with lamb's-quarter leaves, you can quickly steam or sauté them—just make sure not to leave them on the heat for too long, since they're delicate leaves that will break down when overcooked! Lamb's-quarter can be found in North and South America, Hawaii, Africa, Australia, and many northern countries.

- **Amaranth:** Not only are these plants beautiful, but they're doubly useful for foragers. In spring and summer, amaranth leaves can be harvested and cooked. During summer and fall, though, is when amaranth really shines. This is the time of year when amaranth seeds come out, which is exciting news for foragers. Amaranth seeds are very nutritious and can be made into flour, used in all kinds of recipes, and basically used the same as any other ancient grain (think quinoa and farro). Amaranth can be found on every continent except Antarctica.

- **Mulberry**: This popular tree produces some particularly tasty berries that are sure to please any goblin forager. A ripe mulberry will appear mostly black with a hint of red. Once you start spotting mulberries of this color, it's time to get harvesting! You'll be glad to have a supply of these delicious berries, as they can be used in all kinds of ways. Use them to make berry cobbler, jam, smoothies, pie, sorbet, muffins, and more. Best of all, these berries can be found easily in cities. Time to get foraging! Mulberry trees can be found in most of North America, South America, South Asia, and southern Africa.

DANDELION OIL

Whether you want to relieve muscle pain or relax a busy mind, dandelion oil has lots of great everyday uses. Just remember, this recipe isn't for eating! Dandelion oil is only for topical use. (If you want to eat your dandelions, try making them into tea, jelly, or wine.) If you want to make an oil out of something other than dandelions, just use this process but replace dandelions with the dried herb or flower of your choice.

WHAT YOU'LL NEED

- ★ Enough dandelions to fill your container
- ★ A lidded glass jar or container
- ★ Olive oil, or the shelf-stable oil of your choice
- ★ A butter knife, chopstick, or similar utensil
- ★ A piece of cloth
- ★ A rubber band or string

WHAT TO DO

1. Start by foraging your dandelions from a spot that hasn't been treated with herbicide or insecticide. Pick dandelions that are blooming and yellow.

2. Once you bring your dandelions home, give them a good wash. Cut off the dandelion heads and run them under cold water in a colander, then let them sit in a large bowl of water for about 10 minutes, stirring occasionally with your hand.

3. Wilt your dandelions to dry them out a bit: Place your dandelion heads on a towel and cover them lightly with a paper towel. Leave them out overnight.

4. Place your dandelions in your container. Pour your oil over them until they're covered (ideally leaving about ¼ inch of headspace between the top of your oil and the top of your container).

5. Use the butter knife to gently poke your oil and release any air bubbles.

6. Cover the mouth of your container with your cloth, and use a rubber band to secure it. Place your container in a sunny location and let it sit for 2 weeks. Be careful not to leave it for much longer than that, or your oil may start to mold.

7. After the 2 weeks have passed, strain out the dandelion heads and pour the oil into a clean jar. When covered (with a regular lid) and stored in a cool, dry place, your oil will last for up to a year.

Edible and Medicinal Plants 101

Now that you've got a good collection of foraged plants in your kitchen, you might be wondering what to do next. Lucky for you, there are tons of ways to use your foraged goods. From cooking to preserving to making infusions and tinctures, your carefully collected plants can go a long way.

First, make sure to determine which plants are edible and which are medicinal—you'll be unhappy with the flavor of a raw yarrow salad, and a poultice of mulberries is only going to dye you purple. (Some plants, like plantains and dandelions, are both!) Once you've made that determination, carefully clean your plants. You don't want bugs or dirt getting in the way of a delicious meal. Also, check if your plants need extra processing before they're safe to consume (for example, acorns should be leached before they're cooked). Once you've double-checked your research and your foraged finds, you're good to start using them however you see fit.

If you don't want to use all your plants right away, the easiest way to quickly preserve them is to pop them in an airtight zipper storage bag and put them in your freezer. Write the name of the plant, the date you packaged it, and, if you want, any processing you need to do after unpacking the bag (like if you haven't leached your plant yet). When filling the bag, try to lay your plants in a relatively flat layer. It's easier to make sure the storage bag is airtight if it's not bulky. Then, just use your mouth to suck all the air out of the bag, seal it, and put it in your freezer. You're done! Your foraged goods should last for a few weeks like this. With this quick preservation method under your belt, hopefully you'll feel confident enough to try lots of the following techniques for using your foraged finds.

DRYING

Whether you want to make your own tea, or you just want to preserve your foraged foods to make them last longer, learning to dry your foods is a great skill for any foraging goblin to have. As a bonus, it's really easy to do. First, you may want to blanch your food (give it a quick boil, then submerge it in ice water) to ensure it retains more of its color and flavor. After that, you have a few options. For fruits and larger vegetables, slice them relatively thin (they don't have to be paper-thin, but try to get them below ¼ inch thick). Set your oven heat as low as it will go, ideally around 140 degrees Fahrenheit, and place your slices on a baking tray. Put the tray in the oven, and get ready to wait. It'll likely take your food at least 8 hours to dry in an oven, but make sure to check on your food regularly!

For herbs, the drying process is even easier. Just wash your herbs, then tie them into a little bouquet and hang them upside down in a dry place out of direct sunlight to air-dry. This process will take a few days, so it's a good idea to put the herbs in a paper bag to avoid dust, dirt, or bugs congregating on your drying plant. Plants that are particularly good for drying include lavender, rosemary, sage, and thyme. These are all hardy herbs that are unlikely to mold quickly and can stand up to being hung dry for days.

Once your foods are dry, store them in a cool, dry, dark area in an airtight container. Now your foraged goods should last for months!

PRESERVES AND JAMS

Don't be put off by the task of making your own preserves—it's deceptively simple and wildly rewarding. All you need is fruit, sugar, jars, and time. This process will keep your foraged goods safe for over a year if you preserve them correctly. Before you start, make sure to wash your jars (hand-washing or running them through a dishwasher will do). Next, measure how many pounds of foraged finds you want to make into jam. A rough rule of thumb is to use as many cups of sugar as you have pounds of fruit, although it's easy to find jam recipes that will offer more specific amounts. Pour the fruit and sugar into a pot, and stir constantly over low heat until the mixture begins to firm up. Once that happens, pour your jam into jars. It's a good idea to boil the jars (completely submerged, full of jam, with the lids on) for about ten minutes in order to seal the jars closed. For preserves, the process is basically the same— the difference between jam, jelly, and preserves is about the thickness of the final product and how much fruit is in the jar (jelly is made from just fruit juice, jam is bits of fruit mashed up, and preserves use whole fruits or large chunks of fruit). Of course there are lots more tips and tricks to making your own jam, but hopefully you can see now that it's not a difficult task. It's a great way for foraging goblins to spend the day!

Some fruits that are particularly good for jam and preserves are apples, plums, blackberries, citrus fruits, currants, cranberries, and gooseberries. That's because all these fruits have naturally high pectin levels, and pectin is what causes preserves to firm up when you cook them.

TINCTURES AND EXTRACTS

If you're trying to get the most out of your medicinal plants, making tinctures is a great idea. This process draws out all the good, healing properties of your plant into an extract that can be dropped into tea or other beverages, or taken straight. Turning your medicinal plants into tinctures will also make them last longer. One thing to note is that technically a tincture is made using alcohol as the solvent; you use such a small amount of a tincture at a time that the alcohol content is negligible, but if you don't want any alcohol at all you can try vinegar instead. (This is an extract, not a tincture, since tinctures only use alcohol.)

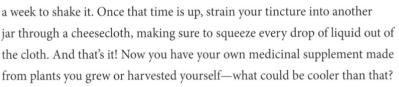

You can use fresh or dried plants to make a tincture. Start by chopping up your plant into very small pieces. Put your chopped plants in a jar, making sure they fill up about half the jar. Then, fill your jar the rest of the way with alcohol, ideally a neutral-tasting spirit such as vodka. Put the lid tightly on your jar, and let your mixture sit for at least 6 to 8 weeks, making sure to check on it once a week to shake it. Once that time is up, strain your tincture into another jar through a cheesecloth, making sure to squeeze every drop of liquid out of the cloth. And that's it! Now you have your own medicinal supplement made from plants you grew or harvested yourself—what could be cooler than that?

Plants that are good to use for tinctures include ginger, feverfew, chamomile, valerian, gingko, milk thistle, and St. John's wort. These are all very useful medicinal plants with a range of uses, and popping a drop or two of any of them into your nighttime tea could give you a boost the next day.

POULTICES

This is probably the easiest way to use your medicinal plants. A poultice is just a mash of plants that you apply to your skin to help heal a wound, calm inflammation, relieve muscle pain, or create any similar effect. To make a poultice, simply pick which plant from your foraged bounty would best help your current ailment, then mash up the plant with a bit of warm or cold water and apply it to the problem area. If you apply the herbs directly to your skin, you can cover them with some gauze to hold them in place. If you want to get a little fancy with your poultice, you can fill a clean cloth (or even a clean sock) with herbs, soak the cloth in water, mash up the herbs inside, and hold the cloth to your wound. It's super easy to use your medicinal plants to make a poultice, so try it next time you're struggling with inflammation or pain and see if it helps!

Here are some good plants to use in your poultice: ginger, turmeric, aloe vera, eucalyptus, and dandelion. These plants all have medicinal effects that would be useful in poultices for anti-inflammatory reasons, arthritis relief, and relief from abrasion pain.

Foraging is perhaps the fastest and most rewarding way to get in touch with nature. It creates an exchange between you and the natural world that isn't some capitalist transaction but rather a genuine sharing of care and understanding. In the modern world, it can be hard to find places to interact with nature directly, but foraging gives us an opportunity to find true intimacy with nature. Once you start harvesting, you'll start noticing the seasons more, start changing your meals a little based on the weather or time of year, start noticing when certain plants are thriving and when they aren't. Suddenly, you're tuned into the cycles of the world that we've become so distanced from in an age where strawberries can be found at the grocery store year-round.

Be respectful of the nature that you forage in. Make sure to look up best practices for harvesting, keep your practice clean and sustainable, and don't take more than you need of anything. Once you get good, start teaching others what you know. Create a community of forage-happy goblins who love living off the land in whatever small way they can. Share the wealth with the people you care about. Treat foraging as an act of love—toward the environment, yourself, and the people around you.

CHAPTER 7

Mud Bath

Self-care doesn't
have to be pretty

It's no secret that the beauty and wellness industries aren't exactly on your side. Rather than focus on accepting and caring for your body, these industries are more determined to "improve" you and keep you striving for a beauty goal that's always out of reach. If you're tired of thinking of your body as a product to be consumed or a goal to be attained, the principles of goblinhood can help. Being a goblin is all about escaping the claws of capitalism (to the extent that anyone can), and that includes pushing back on the beauty/wellness industrial complex and rethinking what self-care means to you.

Goblins care for themselves because it feels good and they deserve it. Goblins care for themselves in ways that genuinely benefit their mental health. Goblins care for themselves in ways that are weird and sometimes a little gross, but who cares! Goblin self-care isn't a performance for others but a private ceremony in praise of their own minds and bodies. Goblin self-care isn't about buying special products or temporarily beating burnout in order to keep grinding. It's about creating positive habits to remind yourself that you matter, that you deserve rest, that your worth lies far outside your productivity. Start making time for goblin self-care and see how your view of yourself changes.

Another important piece of goblin self-care is escaping the search for perfection. Rather than trying to fix yourself or your body, begin to accept the things about you that are different, imperfect, or neglected. This won't be an overnight change. Body image and mental health are struggles that can last a lifetime. No one expects you to wake up tomorrow full of perfect self-acceptance and self-love. But practicing small self-care habits regularly can make a difference in the way you feel about yourself over time. Maybe someday you'll realize that the parts of you that don't perfectly conform to beauty standards—the weird, uncomfortable, "ugly" parts—are valuable in their own right.

Goblin Spa Day

When you think about self-care, you probably conjure up images of sparkling bottles of face wash, expensive moisturizers, women in white bathrobes with cucumbers over their eyes, and glittering hair salons. Maybe you love these images, but maybe they never felt real or accessible to you. If you want to indulge in self-care but you've always felt unsure about the self-care industrial complex, you're not alone. It can be overwhelming to pick through the hundreds of popular skincare products and the thousands of items you supposedly need in order to take care of yourself. Luckily, goblin self-care isn't about a capitalist idea of wellness, nor is it centered on making yourself look better. Goblin spa days are all about self-love: checking in with yourself, spending time with yourself, and feeling better.

Making time to relax and care for yourself can be a huge mood-booster, and it's a great reminder that you're worth caring about! You don't need to buy fancy new products or fixate on improving your looks—you can simply give yourself time to be with yourself, to check in with your body and remember that you deserve to feel good. Whether you spend a few minutes or a whole day indulging in physical self-care, you're sure to feel better after. Here are some tips for honoring your goblin side while also pampering yourself.

EMBRACE THE HOMEMADE: Make your own face masks, body scrubs, and soothing bath ingredients to make your me time that much more personal. Face masks can be made from egg whites, coffee grounds, aloe vera, honey, and more. Body and lip scrubs are easy to make with a bit of sugar and honey. Pour some oatmeal, baking soda, or epsom salt into your bath, along with a few drops of lavender oil. Top everything off with the classic cucumbers over your eyes, and you have a relaxing, homemade spa day.

GET STRANGE WITH SKINCARE: Washing your face can be as weird as you want. One way to embrace goblin skincare is to keep an eye out for face products that use snail slime—yes, snail slime. Snail mucin works great as a moisturizer, and it's said to make skin more hydrated and plumper. If your skin has a bad reaction to snail slime, or if you need more intense moisture, you can always try slugging. Slugging is supposed to be great for dry skin and it's both simple and slightly gross (perfect for goblins). To slug, just apply a layer of petroleum jelly to your face after your nightly face wash. You might have to sleep on a towel, but in the morning your skin should be glowing. If you want an even easier goblin skincare tip, try using acne stickers when you get pimples. Acne stickers are exactly what they sound like—cute little stickers that contain an acne-healing gel. These stickers come in all shapes and colors, and what's a more goblin way to get rid of pimples than covering your face with a fun collection of pretty things?

MAKE YOUR OWN MAKEUP: Nobody should feel like they need to wear makeup, but if you think it's fun to change up your look, there are lots of natural ways to do it. Use beet juice as lip and cheek stain. Mix coconut oil and cocoa powder to make your own brow filler. Rice flour and turmeric or saffron will create a bright, fun eyeshadow. Crush up a bowl of blueberries and use the juice to dye your hair lavender. There are tons of natural ingredients that you can use for a fun goblin makeover.

THINK SUSTAINABLE: The beauty industry creates a lot of waste, so your physical self-care routine is a great place to start thinking sustainably. If there are beauty products you'd rather buy than make, be thoughtful about which items you purchase. Look for organic nail polish, since regular nail polish has a lot of chemicals that are bad for the environment. Spend some time researching brands and products that are eco-friendly. Find makeup brushes made from bamboo instead of plastic. Thinking sustainably can also save money. Instead of buying single-use cotton balls, find some washcloths that you can cut up and wash after use. And of course, making your own products is always going to be better for the environment than buying something.

The Benefits of Wallowing

Have you ever noticed that the word *wallow* can be used to describe lying in the mud, taking pleasure in something, or getting deep in your feelings? Being in a bad mood or in the most indulgent bed of your life use the same verb: the one that means rolling around like a pig in a puddle. Maybe there's a way to bring the same joy we get from luxuriating or getting dirty to our darker feelings. What if, instead of letting difficult feelings overwhelm us, we tried sinking deep into their sticky, swampy depths and let ourselves feel good by feeling bad?

It can be cathartic to let the emotions that we normally suppress bubble up to the surface without judging them or trying to contain them. You don't need to let these feelings take over your life, but being able to recognize and accept them instead of stomping them back down is a skill worth practicing. Rolling around in the mud is a joyful act of embracing the soggier aspects of life—and so is rolling around in your feelings. Treat your pain with the same tenderness you'd treat the tadpole you found in a puddle and get ready to wallow.

1. The first step to wallowing is getting comfortable. Nobody can be expected to properly wallow in an uncomfortable setting. Grab some blankets, put on comfy clothes, settle in on your bed or your couch, and dim the lights. Take a few minutes to create a cozy space for yourself, a space that you'll be comfortable sitting in for a while. Sometimes it's tough to find the energy to do this when you're feeling down, but it'll be worth it to at least put on your pajamas.

2. Make sure you have food available. Nothing throws off a good wallow sesh like an empty stomach. Order a pizza, stock up on frozen meals, or have a friend bring over some snacks. Your food doesn't need to be top-tier and complicated to make, but you need to have something around. If you get too hungry, you'll have a harder time keeping control and perspective. You want to feel your feelings, not let them overpower you.

3. Remember that life can wait. Whether you need an evening, a day, or a weekend of wallowing, remind yourself that you deserve that time. Doing nothing can sometimes feel stressful, since we're so trained to be productive with every minute of our days. But almost anything you think you need to do, whether it's responding to emails or texting people back or doing the dishes, can wait a few days. (Do keep any animals or humans you're in charge of fed and clean, or make arrangements for someone else to do it.) Whatever work you have will be there once you're done wallowing, and hopefully you'll have more energy to face it.

4. Don't worry about cleaning. Your household chores can wait, bathing can wait, everything that's nonessential can wait. Wallowing is not a performance. It's not about looking good while feeling bad. It's purely for you,

and if you need to be dirty and let dust bunnies collect for a few days, then that's what you need to do.

5. Treat yourself with tenderness. This is the most important part of wallowing. It's what distinguishes wallowing from a regular depressive episode. Rather than spending your wallowing time steeped in self-hatred and self-doubt, take that time to instead examine your emotions. Why did you need to take this time to wallow? What emotions have come up since you've been wallowing? What thoughts or feelings have you been returning to during this time? Whatever emotions come up, try not to get angry at yourself for having them or shove them back down. Instead, allow yourself to feel those feelings, to offer care and attention to both easy and difficult emotions. Sometimes this feels bad. Be prepared for that. But offering yourself tenderness will ultimately help you far more than it hurts. You deserve to be treated with care and thoughtfulness, even when you're not feeling your best.

6. Emerge from the wallow. Eventually, you'll need to come out of it—it's a bummer but it's true. However, you don't need to do it all at once. Start slowly, by taking a shower or texting a friend just to say hi. Maybe cook yourself a simple meal if you're feeling ambitious. If you're returning to work, spend your first day back working a little slower than you normally would. Take a walk, or visit a place that's outside your lair but still makes you feel safe and comfortable. Remember that you have friends and a support group. There's no need to jump out of your wallow back into your regular life at your regular speed. Continue being careful with yourself and your emotions, and move at the speed that feels best to you. Remember the lessons you learned while you were wallowing.

UNGGUE

◇

Please note that this section is not for the faint of heart, or weak of stomach. We're about to dive into something pretty gross.

In Sir Terry Pratchett's classic Discworld series, goblins practice a religion called Unggue. It's based on the principle that bodily leavings and secretions are sacred and should be cared for and preserved. The goblins practice this religion by making small, beautiful pots and filling the pots with secretions: all the earwax, fingernail and toenail clippings, and snot that leave their bodies over the course of their lives. The Discworld goblins spend their lives filling their pots with their special parts and fluids so that they can be buried with everything their bodies have ever produced. Goblins are not popular on the Discworld.

It's fair to say that, while gross, Pratchett's goblin religion seems to be getting at something that's rarely discussed. What it's getting at is this: Living things are gross. People are gross. We're made of oozing, gooey fibers and membranes. We're filled with pus and phlegm. We fester and scab and puke and seep. What could be grosser than that? What could possibly be more foul and disgusting than the human body?

And yet, this nastiness is what allows us to live. People are gross all the way down, but we're all equally gross, and we're all gross for a reason. We need earwax and snot and fingernails in order to live. Organs are icky goo sacks, but you would die without the icky goo sacks that are your brain, heart, lungs, and more.

Maybe Unggue is a reminder that we can accept, and even love, the gross parts of ourselves. Everyone is gross. What if we started celebrating, or at least accepting, the gross stuff? (Maybe not collecting it, though.)

If our bodies are worth caring for, then *all* parts of our bodies are worth caring for. Unggue is a lesson in embracing every part of yourself, in assigning care and meaning to even the parts that you'd rather ignore. Even the parts that are often considered ugly or weird.

Chill Scents to Relax and Study To

Smells have the power to bring back memories, trigger strong emotions, and change our mood. Smell is the sense that's most connected to memory, which is why we tend to have strong emotional reactions to various scents and why smelling something familiar can suddenly bring back a long-buried memory. If you're feeling down, certain smells can brighten your mood, make you feel calm, or give you energy. So why not start working scent into your self-care routine?

Aromatherapy and essential oils have become hugely popular, and not without reason. Because scent is so closely twined to memories and emotions, it makes sense that harnessing the power of smells would be useful for changing your mental state. There are lots of ways to work smell into your self-care routine and many aromatherapy methods that you can make yourself. Essential oils are difficult to make on your own, but you can make infused oils (check out page 174 for a how-to), fragrance sachets, lightly scented lotions, and fragrance sticks all by yourself without much hassle. And if you make

your own scented items, you get to choose exactly which smells to use. Experiment to find out which scents smell best to you and which have the biggest effect on your mood. If you're not sure where to start, here's a simple guide on scents and their emotional effects.

- **For sleep**: Chamomile, sweet marjoram, cedar.

- **For waking up**: Coffee, rosemary, peppermint.

- **For relaxing**: Lavender, pine, bergamot.

- **For boosting your mood**: Citrus, sandalwood, freshly cut grass.

- **For improving focus**: Thyme, cinnamon, sage.

- **For pain relief**: Apple, lemongrass, clary sage.

Making your own scented items is generally better than buying essential oils, since the latter aren't regulated by the FDA and can contain harmful chemicals. If you do buy essential oils, research the company you're buying from. And remember: essential oils are really bad for pets! Never put essential oils in a diffuser or humidifier if you have a pet.

FRAGRANCE STONES

Looking for a goblin-friendly way to fill your home with goblin-friendly scents? Make some fragrance stones! Nothing says goblin like scattering scented, homemade rocks around your space. The great thing about making your own fragrance stones is that you get to choose whatever smells you like best. Maybe you want your space to smell musky and sweet, or earthy and fresh. Maybe you want to smell rain or pine trees all day. Maybe you even want your fragrance stones to smell like, well, stones. The power is in your hands.

WHAT YOU'LL NEED

- ★ 1½ cups white flour, plus more as needed
- ★ ¼ cup salt
- ★ ¼ teaspoon cornstarch
- ★ ⅔ cup boiling water, plus more as needed
- ★ 1 tablespoon essential oil or infused oil
- ★ Food coloring (optional)
- ★ 2 tablespoons dried herbs, flower petals, or citrus rinds (optional)

WHAT TO DO

1. To make your own infused oils, follow the directions for making dandelion oil (page 174) but substitute the herb or flower of your choice.

2. In a bowl, combine the flour, salt, and cornstarch.

3. Slowly add the boiling water to the mixture, stirring constantly.

4. Once the mixture cools, use your hands to knead the dough until it's firm. Add more flour if the dough is too wet, or more water if it's too dry. The dough should be smooth, firm, and not too sticky.

5. Add oil. If you're using food coloring, add that now as well.

6. Knead in the oil until evenly combined. If you're using food coloring, knead until the color is evenly dispersed.

7. Once the oil is mixed in, pinch off small (1- to 2-inch) pieces of dough. Roll the dough in your hands into a ball, and then shape it into a stone. You can press dried herbs or flowers on top if you want.

8. Place stones on a baking sheet or cooling rack and let them dry for at least 8 hours.

9. Place the stones in bowls or jars around your lair to scent your space. If their smell starts wearing off, just add a few more drops of oil to them.

Meditate on It

Whether you struggle with anxiety, find yourself easily distracted, or just appreciate a calm moment in a busy world, creating a space in your lair for mindfulness and meditation will help you more than you can imagine. Regularly practicing meditation can help lower anxiety and stress, keep you present and focused throughout the day, help manage difficult emotions, and even improve creativity. All it takes is setting aside a few minutes every day to practice mindfulness and give your busy brain a break.

To encourage yourself to meditate, and to make your meditations particularly positive experiences, it can be useful to create a meditation space for yourself. This is an area—it could be a room, a closet, or a corner—that's specifically designed to make you feel calm and relaxed. For most people, meditation spaces are minimalist and empty. However, don't worry if you're someone who prefers more to less. Your meditation space only needs to be relaxing to you. Being surrounded by carefully chosen clutter can make you feel more grounded and remind you of what you love. What's going to make you feel more calm then being surrounded by some of your favorite things? If you're someone who doesn't feel at home in an empty space, then don't meditate in an empty space! Make your meditation area feel cozy in whatever way you choose to define coziness. It's going to be easier to relax and focus if you feel safe and comfortable.

What type of space is cluttered, cozy, relaxing, and natural? The answer is simple: a forest. Making your meditation area feel like a forest will connect you to both nature and yourself. After all, what's more calming than imagining sitting on a patch of moss in a shady wood? Forests aren't minimalist or clean; they're filled with mushrooms and pine needles and birds and stumps and flowers and shadows and all kinds of bugs. They're calming, cluttered wonderlands where we can get in touch with the natural world in all its weird, muddy glory. Here are some tips for bringing the meditative power of a forest into your lair.

Find your space. The first step to making your meditation space is, of course, finding a space. If you're in a home or a larger apartment, you might have a whole room that can become a forest meditation room. If you don't have that much extra real estate, pick a corner that you don't use much and assign that as your meditation space. If you choose a meditation space one day and decide the next day that it isn't working, that's fine. Sometimes it takes trial and error to pick the right spot. However, reserving a particular place for mindfulness is going to encourage you to practice, and it can be meaningful to designate a part of your space solely to caring for your mind.

Don't meditate alone. When we think of meditation, we often think of sitting silently with our thoughts for minutes on end. That's a tough way to meditate if you're a beginner. Instead, try downloading a free meditation app (there are tons), podcast, or video that you enjoy. It can take a bit to find a meditation you like to listen to, but it's worth the effort. Guided meditation is a great way to learn the basics, and if you decide to use meditation to work through a specific issue or concern, guided meditation can be a huge help. Don't convince yourself that you need to meditate in silence in order to "do it right." Do whatever works best for you!

Involve all your senses. To make a space that feels truly calming, you'll need to go beyond how your meditation space looks. You also want smells, textures, and sounds that will help you relax and focus. Because this is a forest-themed meditation space, try using scents like pine, cedar, and peppermint to evoke a woodsy environment while also promoting relaxation and thoughtfulness. Besides your meditation guide, bring in other sounds that make you feel relaxed and connected to nature. Queue up a playlist of rain sounds or find a video of forest noises. Play the sounds quietly enough that they calm you without being distracting. For textures, try bringing in a rug or blankets that remind you of the soft soil of the forest floor, or pillows with the velvety texture of moss.

Keep it light. Light is an important part of meditation. It'll be harder to feel present if you're sitting under an intense fluorescent bulb, so make sure to take into account what type of light makes you feel calm. To section your meditation space off from the light in the rest of your room, try hanging a sheet from your ceiling like a canopy. This will allow you to light your space however you want without any bright overhead lights interfering. To mimic the dim or dappled light of a forest, try laying strands of fairy lights around your space. You could also bring in salt lamps or dimmable table lamps to add to the atmosphere. Lighting seems like a small detail, but it'll go a long way in calming your mind.

Get comfy and calm. It's hard to feel relaxed if you're uncomfortable. Prioritize comfort in your meditation space by bringing in pillows, cushions, blankets, and rugs. If your space feels comfortable, you're more likely to spend time in it. Ideally your meditation space is a spot where you feel safe and serene. For a forest meditation space, try bringing in cushions and pillows of different textures and densities to mimic the diversity of plants, roots, rocks, and tree trunks in the woods. Cover the ground in rugs and blankets that remind you of the overgrown forest floor.

Decorate your forest. Some people say it's important to have an uncluttered meditation space, and it's true that you don't want your space to feel messy and distracting. However, for goblins it can be nice to have some positive clutter. Decorations can make your space feel more personal, which will likely make you feel more relaxed. There's nothing wrong with having a meditation space with lots of decorations as long as you don't feel distracted. A forest-themed meditation space might include decor such as plants, crystals, jars of dirt, dark green and brown cushions and blankets, dried flowers, and decorative branches. It might take time to decorate your meditation nook in a way that feels both personal and relaxing, but once you strike the right balance, you'll never want to leave your mindfulness spot.

Cultivate a Goblin Crew

What can mushrooms and fungus teach us about friendship? Well, like mushrooms growing together in a fairy ring, friends stick by each other, support each other, and help each other grow. Friendship is the complex, unknowable, essential fungus that connects us all. Even though you might sometimes feel alone, having friends means you can be sure that you're always connected to a support system. Friends nourish each other, raise each other up, and connect each other to a larger world. When mushrooms grow in a ring, they're actually all part of the same organism. When we make friends, we also join together and become something bigger than ourselves.

It's great to be an introvert or enjoy your alone time, but eventually everyone needs the love and support that friendship offers. Finding good friends and learning to be a good friend are skills that will serve you for the rest of your life. Learning to be a friend will teach you empathy, patience, thoughtfulness, how to love yourself and others, and so much more. If you're feeling down, having friends means you'll always have people to care for you. If your friend is struggling, you can learn to care for others. Keep in mind all the great things that friendship can offer you as you set off in search of a goblin crew.

Making friends isn't always easy, though, especially if (like many goblins) you've often been seen as weird. Here are some ideas for attracting and curating your goblin band.

Go online. This is the most obvious place to find fellow goblins. You can find anything online, and that includes goblin friends. There are goblincore communities on every social networking site—TikTok, Twitter, Tumblr, Reddit, Discord—and they're all pretty active, too. Join a subreddit or get on TikTok and start chatting with your goblin community.

> Be careful about sharing your personal information online. This advice sounds old and tired, but it's still true. You never really know who you're talking to, and you never know where your personal information might end up. Don't let that scare you away from joining online goblincore communities, just make sure you're being safe and smart and keeping your personal information private.

Join a club. There are probably more clubs in your community than you're aware of. Therefore, it's likely that at least a few of these clubs will align with your interests. Look for groups that go on hikes together or groups that spend weekends getting rid of invasive plants. Maybe your library has a themed book club you can join, or maybe there's a crafting club that your local craft store knows about. Join a community garden, a bird-watching club, or even an online rock-collecting group. You don't need to find a club that encompasses all of your goblin interests, but finding a group of people who share your passion for at least one of your interests will almost definitely result in a goblin friend.

Sign up for a class. This is like joining a club, with the added bonus that you get to learn a skill. Your local library probably offers a lot of classes on all kinds of things, so that's a great place to start looking. If there's a botanical garden, museum, or university near you, these can also be great places to take classes. Check out classes on goblin-y topics like botanical drawing, basket weaving, ice fishing, pickling, making and using natural dyes, assemblage jewelry, home composting, and more to increase the likelihood that you'll meet other goblins. Learning a new skill alongside strangers can feel scary at first, but it's actually a great bonding experience. Everyone in your class probably feels the same way you do, and being honest with one of your classmates about how you're feeling is a great way to create a connection with someone. Find a class that aligns with your interests and you're sure to find a goblin friend.

Organize goblin events. If you're feeling enterprising, you can always organize your own goblin events. This is a great way to lure the goblins in your community right to your doorstep. Try hosting events like potluck picnics at your local park, a recycled goods craft night, a marathon of your favorite goblincore movies, a clothing swap, or a tabletop roleplaying game night. Invite your existing friends and tell them to bring other people who might be interested, or advertise your event around your community. There are definitely other goblins near you who are also looking for goblin friends, and will be thrilled to hear about your event.

Once you find your fellow goblins, how do you make connections? The hardest part of making a new friend is talking to someone for the first time. It can feel weird and awkward, but it's always going to be worth it if you come out of one uncomfortable conversation with a great friend. Even though it can feel overwhelming to make connections, there are lots of useful tips and strategies to keep in mind that will make it easier to make new friends.

Be honest. Honesty is a way of embracing our imperfections. If you can be honest with someone about your vulnerabilities, you're showing that you accept your own flaws and foibles—at least enough that you won't be judgmental of flaws and foibles in others. Starting a conversation with a small confession, maybe about how you were nervous to talk to this person or join this club, or how you're not sure about how your craft project is turning out. You don't need to overshare (and try to resist being self-deprecating), but chances are whoever you're talking to is also feeling nervous. By opening a conversation with your own honesty, you're allowing the other person space to be honest in return. You're creating room for both of you to embrace your imperfections.

Give compliments. Once you practice seeing beauty everywhere, you'll probably become really good at giving compliments. After all, everyone has something unique or cool or beautiful about them, whether it's a fun pin, a brightly colored bag, a crocheted hat, or something less immediately obvious, like a great sense of humor or impressive cooking abilities. Nothing will help someone warm up to you faster than giving them a genuine compliment, so start paying attention to that beauty and make yourself a friend! (Until you know someone very well, it's a good idea to confine your comments to things they can control—stuff like their personality traits, skills, and style choices— not any part of their body, even if they have *really* beautiful eyes.)

Ask questions. Being a good community member means thinking of other people, and a great way to show that you're thinking of other people is by asking questions. Asking new friends questions will show that you're interested in them and that you care about them. If you have an opportunity to make someone feel special and cared for, why not take it? Pay attention to the things your new friend likes, dislikes, and has interesting thoughts about, and ask them to expand on those things. Follow up about events, ideas, and recommendations they mention. Make sure they know that you value them as much as they value you, because that's what being a good community member is all about.

Find common ground. Did you know that getting cozy goes beyond physically feeling cozy? You can get cozy in a conversation by finding common ground with your new friend. Steering the conversation toward things you both enjoy can keep the conversation from becoming awkward or one-sided. If you want to start feeling comfortable around someone, finding common ground is a quick way to do that, whether you find your commonalities by asking questions, offering topics you're interested in, or even noticing things about your new friend that might shed a light on their interests (like a T-shirt they're wearing or a book they're carrying). Finding a subject you both care about is a great way to find comfort with a new person.

Remember that almost everyone wants friends. When you talk to someone new, it can be easy to feel like you're the only person in the world looking for new friends. But that's just not true. Finding like-minded people who understand and nurture you is an incredibly empowering experience, and most people are on the lookout for this kind of empowerment. When you meet a new friend, remind yourself that they're as interested as you are in everything friendship can offer. Keep this in mind, and you'll be surprised just how often you notice that other people seem glad you want to be friends.

Self-care means much more than washing your face or taking a bath every now and then. It's about making sure that you're prioritizing your mental health, tending to your body's needs, and seeking out happiness regularly. Self-care won't look the same to everyone, and that's okay. Everyone wants and needs different things. Take the time to find out what self-care means to you, whether it's working in your pollinator-friendly flower garden, taking walks on the beach after dark, making time to read through your collection of books on folklore, or actually taking a mud bath.

Ultimately, self-care is about reminding yourself that you deserve a place in this world, and steadily eking that place out for yourself. Sometimes life gets overwhelming, and it can be hard to remember that you need to watch after yourself, too. But the more time you spend being kind to yourself and finding empowerment, the better you'll feel, and the more you'll be able to offer others. Caring for yourself is a radical act because it means you belong in the world.

Go Forth and Goblin

The world as it stands is generally more interested in conformity and assimilation than in personal comfort and style. Goblincore is particularly suited for folks who have always felt out of place in a world that doesn't want to make space for them. Embracing a goblin lifestyle means embracing all the things that make you different, and realizing that those are the coolest and best things about you. Hopefully, embracing your goblinness can make you feel seen and remind you that no matter how you choose to live your life, there's a community behind you and a lot of fun to be had.

No matter your tastes, there are always ways to bring the goblin spirit into your life. Whether you live in a shoebox studio apartment or a house in the suburbs or even a converted school bus, you can invite comfort and greenery into your space in order to make it perfect for you. Whether you prefer wearing skirts or jeans, sneakers or high heels, homemade sweaters or store-bought hoodies, you can prioritize wearing clothes that make you feel good. This is what the goblin lifestyle is all about: reclaiming personal comfort and style to remind yourself that you belong in this world, even if the world seems determined to exclude you.

Honoring our goblin selves means celebrating our passions, asserting our right to green spaces, listening to our bodies, watching the world with curiosity, and prioritizing comfort. It also reminds us to collect cool rocks, respect bugs, and generally be weirder. If you want to get down and dirty, goblins invite you into the mud and muck and mushrooms. If you're slightly more tidy, you can still be a goblin; your collection of animal bones will just be more organized than the next guy's.

That's why it's good to be a goblin in community with other goblins: there's always someone who loves to do the thing you're not as interested in, and that person can offer a lot of insight into the things you are into. Together, goblins are stronger and stranger than they are apart.

Goblincore is more than just a style of decorating or a call for comfier clothes (although those things are certainly part of it). The goblin life is about making space for your weirdest, soggiest, most unspeakable needs and wants. It's about realizing that even when you're feeling sad and slimy, you still deserve a place in the world. It's about standing up and thoughtfully making room in your bog for other people—all kinds of people, no matter how different they are from you. Being a goblin means looking at the earth, our big ball of mud and dirt, and wondering how you can make it a stranger, muckier, more genuine, more fun place to be. That's what goblin mode is really about.

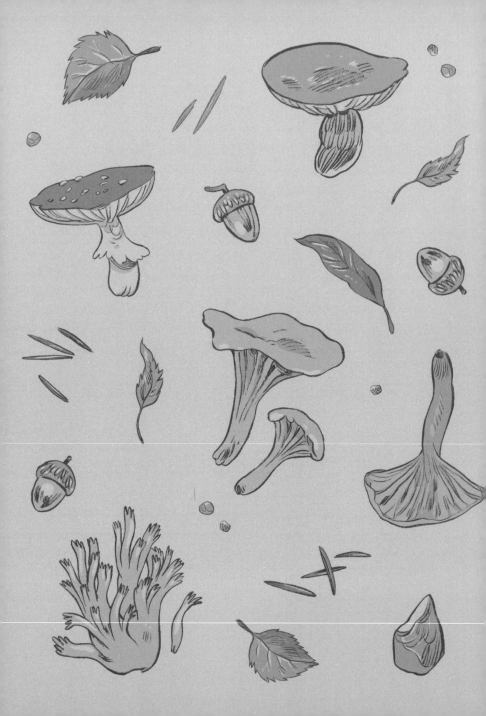